THE THIRD MAN RISING

God's Loving Heart Exposed

by

Scott E. Beemer

Black Forest Press
Mosheim, Tennessee
August 2006
First Edition

THE THIRD MAN RISING

God's Loving Heart Exposed

by

Scott E. Beemer

PUBLISHED IN THE UNITED STATES OF AMERICA
BY
BLACK FOREST PRESS
490 Mountain View Drive
Mosheim, TN 37818

**Cover design
by
Aurora Zhivago**

Scriptures are taken from the New King James Version, copyright 1979, 1982 by Thomas Nelson, Inc. Publishers. Used by permission.

Disclaimer

Printed in the United States of America
Library of Congress
Catalogue-in-Publication

ISBN: 1-58275-178-1

ACKNOWLEDGEMENTS

The Holy Spirit inspired this book.

DEDICATION

To God's Open Forum and the
San Diego First Assembly of God's
"Saints Alive Group."

PROLOGUE

THIS IS A BOOK OF REVELATION ABOUT **MY PLAN FOR MAN**, THE MEN I SEEK, THE MEN I DESIRE, AND THE PLAN MADE PLAIN. THIS WILL COVER A <u>COURSE OF BEGINNINGS</u> [OLD TESTAMENT], <u>MID-POINT CRISES</u> [JESUS], <u>END TIME VICTO-RIES</u> [RAPTURES], THE <u>FINAL EARTH TIME TRAINING</u> [1000 YRS], AND <u>PREPARATIONS FOR ETERNITY</u> OPENING. ALL OF THESE EVENTS CENTERING ON **MAN'S HEART AND ON GOD'S HEART**.

I WILL TAKE THIS TO BE A NEW WAY OF TEACHING AND A DESIRED WAY OF OPENING THE CHILDREN'S EYES. <u>IT IS THE PENETRATING OF THE HEART OF MAN</u> THAT BRINGS OUT THE PROPER RESPONSE FOR ME TO WORK WITH. THERE IS MUCH SAID IN MY WORD ABOUT THE HEART OF MAN AND THIS BOOK SHOULD MAKE MY SCRIPTURES BURST OPEN WITH THE TRUTH REVEALED. MANY NEW POINTS AND AVENUES WILL BE EXPOSED FOR THE SEARCHING ONES TO FIND GOLD. YES, THERE ARE GOLDEN TRUTHS, AND THERE ARE SILVER TRUTHS, AND TRUTHS OF PURE DIRT. IT IS THE TEST OF MAN HOW HE USES THE UNSPOKEN TRUTHS THAT WILL LEAD HIM INTO TRUTHS OF TRUE REVELATION.

WHAT A PATH IS WEAVED FOR EACH PERSON'S LIFE, ALL DIF-FERENT, YET ALL THE SAME. THE SAME FLESH WITH DIFFER-ENT SKINS, THE HEARTS WITH DIFFERENT SEEING, THE SAME HANDS BUT WITH DIFFERENT GRASPS OF THINGS. THEY ARE <u>ALL FACETS OF MINE</u> SHOWING IN THE HEART AND FLESH OF MAN THE VIEWS OF LIFE I DESIRE TO BRING FORTH. NO ONE PATH IS FOR ALL, BUT ALL MUST WALK IN THE SAME KIND OF FLESH IN DIFFERENT PLACES. NEVER DO I SHOW FAVORITES, BUT I HAVE RESPONSIVE LOVED ONES THAT I CAN USE TO MY PLEASING. EVERYONE HAS EQUAL AND PERFECT GOALS SET BEFORE THEM.

NO GOAL IS BETTER OR WORSE THAN ANOTHER. ALL GOALS ARE SET BY THE FATHER AND WATCHED OVER BY ALL THREE.

OUR JOY IS THE RELEASING OF TASKS OF LOVE, AND GUIDING WILLING ONES ON THEIR PATHS OF PURPOSE. YES, <u>WE SET PURPOSES TO BE FULFILLED AND PLANS TO BE PERFECTED</u>. THE TIMING IS A CONTROLLED OVERVIEW OF OUR END DESIRES TO BE ACHIEVED. HOW WE PLAN, AND HOW THE PLAN UNFOLDS, IS PART OF OUR JOY IN WATCHING. ALWAYS KNOWING THE END DOES NOT TAKE AWAY OUR PLEASURE OF PURSUIT OF PERFECTION UNFOLDING.

THE PURPOSEFUL EXECUTION OF THE FATHER'S WILL IS THE ONLY WAY SET FOR OUR CHOSEN ONES. THE FAILURE OF SO MANY IS THE PRICE WE MUST PAY TO GAIN THE BLESSING OF HAVING SO MANY SUCCEED. OUR WEEDING OUT OF UNUSABLES IS <u>PROTECTION FOR ETERNITY DESIRED</u>. THE SUCCESS OF EACH CHILD WON IS A VICTORY CELEBRATED FOREVER.

NEVER FAIL TO APPRECIATE THE WINNING ONES, THE LOW AND THE HIGH, BECAUSE ALL HAVE SECURED A FOREVER WITH THE FATHER. IT IS THE "BEING ONE WITH THE FATHER" THAT BRINGS EVERLASTING LOVE /JOY OF VICTORY. NO WORDS OF WRITTEN WORTH WILL EVER REVEAL ALL THE THINGS HERE REFERRED TO. **ALL,** ***EVERY CHILD OF GOD IN ETERNITY WITH HIM,*** WILL BE HIS FOREVER WITHOUT END, AND ALL HE DOES WILL BE SATISFYING THE CHILDREN'S DESIRES. HIS PLANS ARE ALREADY COMPLETE, BUT THE ETERNAL UNFOLDING IS THE ONLY METHOD OF REVELATION. WHAT A TIME IS SET AHEAD, ONLY LIFE "LIVING IT" WILL EXPLAIN.

LIFT YOUR EYES UP AND LOOK FOR YOUR HELP IN THE REDEEMER. HE HAS MADE A WAY FOR YOU TO DRAW CLOSE TO ALMIGHTY GOD, THE SOURCE OF ALL THINGS. DO NOT LOOK TO MAN OR THE WORLDLY WAYS FOR YOUR DIRECTION. DRAW STRENGTH FROM THE ONE TRUE SOURCE AND EXPERIENCE THE LOVE OF GOD AND HIS BOUNTIFUL BLESSINGS. GIVE UNTO OTHERS WHAT GOD HAS GIVEN TO YOU. BE

A SOURCE OF BLESSINGS, NOT A STAGNANT POOL. LET THE BLESSINGS FLOW INTO YOUR LIFE AND OUT TO BLESS OTH-ERS. GOD HAS A NEVER-ENDING SUPPLY. BE A CHANNEL OF HIS LOVE.

> *"Believe in the Lord your God, and you shall be established; believe His prophets, and you shall prosper."*
> **II Chronicles 20:20**

TABLE OF CONTENTS

CHAPTER ONE

CHAPTER TWO
2000 YEARS, ADAM TO ABRAHAM

CHAPTER THREE
2000 YEARS, ABRAHAM TO JESUS

CHAPTER FOUR
2000 YEARS, JESUS TO ARMAGEDDON

CHAPTER FIVE
1000 YEARS, JUDGMENT TO JUDGMENT

CHAPTER ONE

THE WORDS "MAN RISING" MEANS GOD RISING UP IN MAN IN PLANNED STAGES, GOD ENTERING INTO MEN IN THEIR FLESH, DOING A WORK OF TRANSFORMATION, BRINGING MAN TO A "GOD-LIKE" CONDITION, THUS COMPLETING *"IN HIS IMAGE & LIKENESS"*

THIS BOOK IS CENTERED ON MAN AND GOD'S HEART.

THE BEGINNING

To make a start of anything God always knows the ending. This is reasonable, how else should a start be formed if the assumed end weren't known? What then was God starting? He was setting out to make a family of men to be just like Him. He, God, is One but three separate expressions of Himself at the present time. God's desire was to increase this expression of Himself to something greater than three! He was to become LOVE expanded, LOVE out-reaching, LOVE creating. His LOVE overflowing becoming numerous enough to satisfy LOVE'S planned increase!

The progression of His expression started with one, then was made into a reformable two to become the source of reproducible seed of unknown many. Then the seed became contaminated and cleansing was required by making choosing an act of loving desire. Therefore no seed was an acceptable, returnable seed that wasn't tested, tried, and found with a great desiring love to return to the Oneness from which it came. This then is briefly what God's Bible gives expression to, telling in more detail the plan of God creating His Forever Family, and giving explanation to man about His plan.

THIS BOOK'S GOAL

The goal of this book is to weave through the Bible story, touching on Men's hearts with the purpose of showing how each one won a place with God or how they failed to win God's approval. The reasons shown should point the reader to how they may find their way into the heart of God. Every child of God is different, and God the Father of all is able to receive His children by knowing each ones true heart for Him. Pray and ask that God will expose to you just how your heart should be prepared to find a safe haven in the loving arms of your Abba Father. Come and learn from other's successes and from their failures. Your love of God should grow as you learn about God's own heart, and learn of the boundless Grace of God.

MAN'S HEART*

The first mention of man's heart in the Bible is when God, in His disappointment said,

5 "Then the LORD saw that the wickedness of man *was* great in the earth, and *that* <u>every intent of the thoughts of his heart*</u> *was* only evil continually. 6 And the LORD was sorry that He had made man on the earth, and He was grieved in His heart." Gen. 6:5,6

When speaking of the heart of man this means speaking of his human spirit. This spirit is his connection to God's eternal [Spiritual] realm; and it is placed in the center of his body. The forming of God's likeness required this spirit and a soul [soul, man's mind, will, ego and emotions] then of course these two needed a physical body for containment and operation in the environment that he was to survive in; a body to become the temple of the Holy Spirit. I Cor. 6:19

Man's heart [spirit] was simply his part of God that gave life to the other parts; the blood pump [heart of flesh] conveys this life throughout all of the flesh, that's why man calls it his heart and that's why God says the life is in the blood. In truth it is just a life pump required to support the flesh. The whole life of man on earth is but a schooling place of preparation for his life eternal with God.

23 "Now may the God of peace Himself sanctify you completely; and may your <u>whole spirit, soul, and body</u> be preserved blameless at the coming of our Lord Jesus Christ. 24 He who calls you *is* faithful, who also will do *it*." 1 Thess. 5:23, 24

9 "As for you, my son Solomon, know the God of your father, and serve Him with <u>a loyal heart* and with a willing mind; for the LORD searches all hearts and understands all the intent of the thoughts</u>. If you seek Him, He will be found by you; but if you forsake Him, He will cast you off forever." 1 Chron. 28:9

GOD'S HEART*

The first mention of God's heart in the Bible is when God saw the early fall of man:

5 "Then the LORD saw that the wickedness of man *was* great in the earth, and *that* every <u>intent of the thoughts of his heart</u> *was* only evil continually. 6 And the LORD was sorry that He had made man on the earth, and <u>He was grieved in His heart</u>."* Gen.6:5,6

Was God ever grieved before? These verses are the only ones that touched man' heart and God's heart at the same time. Then God spoke to His own heart in the following scriptures.

20 "Then Noah built an altar to the LORD, and took of every clean animal and of every clean bird, and offered burnt offerings on the altar. 21 And the LORD smelled a soothing aroma. Then the LORD <u>said in His heart</u>,* "I will never again curse the ground for man's sake, although the <u>imagina-</u>

tion of man's heart *is* evil from his youth; nor will I again destroy every living thing as I have done." Gen. 8:20,21*

35 "Then I will raise up for Myself a faithful priest *who* shall do according to what *is* in My heart *and in My mind. I will build him a sure house, and he shall walk before My anointed forever." I Sam. 2:35*

14 "But now your kingdom shall not continue. The LORD has sought for Himself a man after His own heart,* and the LORD has commanded him *to be* commander over His people, because you have not kept what the LORD commanded you." I Sam. 13:14*

In these scriptures you have the clue to man pleasing God, see and learn your lesson for evermore! These *four scriptures are pointing the way in which God Himself operates; this is showing man how he should learn to live and do. No other lesson could be more important for man to know than to understand how God motivates Himself. Man is to follow only what God's heart and mind desires, this then is man's challenge *to grow so close to God that man is only obedient to God's will and way*! *Note these are Not the only scriptures that speak of God's heart, there are a few more, but there are about 558 scriptures that speak of man's heart. Just this is enough to show how important the heart of man is to God!

To understand the men of the Bible the ways of God must be well known. God knows the end from the beginning, because of His overview of all men it will be found that many of the great men of God do not seem to follow, through their life, the basic precepts God demands, however God picks such men because He loved them and He knew their hearts, also they seemed to know something of God's heart. Moses was a murderer, David was an adulterer and murderer, just as examples. So follow God's heart when seeking knowledge of how man should live to gain a place in God's Kingdom.

GOD'S GRACE

God, knowing man's position in earth, realized his love for man would be the only salvation of man. 8 "But Noah found grace in the eyes of the LORD." Gen. 6:8

When the love of God flows out to man it is the release of God's Grace making it so! Grace is a facet of love that compels the heart of God to move in loving action. Grace is a blinder God wears when the seeing of a thing would discourage Him. God's Heart, Love, and Grace are all parts of Him giving expressions of His true self. This picture of God's Grace is given to show the children a direction they are going. It is the outgoing expressions, through Love and Grace, which will combine to make a man the Son of God. It is the flowing of Grace through Love that draws a man to God. Learn Love and Grace will flow, be gracious and love will show.

The grace of God is shown dramatically by Jesus' gift of physical healings to man in Isaiah 53. God's grace is also shown by God's gift of an earth with every requirement for man already provided before he was created. God has already set before man today every blessing he will ever need. It is just up to man to learn how to appropriate what God has already provided.

GOD'S PLAN

God's plan for a family required Him to create a place for their birthing and growing, so came forth the Universe, the Earth and Man in that order.

1"In the beginning <u>God created*</u> the heavens and the earth. 2 The earth was without form, and void; and darkness *was* on the face of the deep. And the Spirit of God was hovering over the face of the waters.

3 Then God said, <u>'Let*</u> there be light'; and there was light. 4 And God saw the light, that *<u>it was </u>*<u>good</u>; and God divided the light from the darkness. 5 God called the light Day, and the darkness He called Night. So the evening and the morning were the first day.

6 Then God said, '<u>Let</u> there be a firmament in the midst of the waters, and <u>let</u> it divide the waters from the waters.' 7 Thus God <u>made*</u> the firmament, and divided the waters which *were* under the firmament from the waters which *were* above the firmament; and it was so. 8 And God called the firmament Heaven. So the evening and the morning were <u>the second day.</u>

9 Then God said, 'Let the waters under the heavens be gathered together into one place, and let the dry *land* appear'; and it was so. 10 And God called the dry *land* Earth, and the gathering together of the waters He called Seas. And God saw that *it was good*.*

11 Then God said, 'Let the earth bring forth grass, the herb *that* yields seed, *and* the fruit tree *that* yields fruit according to its kind, whose seed *is* in itself, on the earth'; and it was so. 12 And the earth brought forth grass, the herb *that* yields seed according to its kind, and the tree *that* yields fruit, whose seed *is* in itself according to its kind. And God saw that *it was good*. 13 So the evening and the morning were the third day.

14 Then God said, 'Let there be lights in the firmament of the heavens to divide the day from the night; and let them be for signs and seasons, and for days and years; 15 and let them be for lights in the firmament of the heavens to give light on the earth'; and it was so. 16 Then God made two great lights: the greater light to rule the day, and the lesser light to rule the night. *He made the stars* also. 17 God set them in the firmament of the heavens to give light on the earth, 18 and to rule over the day and over the night, and to divide the light from the darkness. And God saw that *it was good*. 19 So the evening and the morning were the fourth day.

20 Then God said, 'Let the waters abound with an abundance of living creatures, and let birds fly above the earth across the face of the firmament of the heavens.'

21 So God created great sea creatures and every living thing that moves, with which the waters abounded, according to their kind, and every winged bird according to its kind. And God saw that *it was good*.

22 And God blessed them, saying, 'Be fruitful and multiply, and fill the waters in the seas, and let birds multiply on the earth.' 23 So the evening and the morning were the fifth day.

24 Then God said, 'Let the earth bring forth the living creature according to its kind* cattle and creeping thing and beast of the earth, *each* according to its kind'; and it was so. 25 And God made the beast of the earth according to its kind, cattle according to its kind, and everything that creeps on the earth according to its kind. And God saw that *it was good*

26 Then God said, 'Let Us make man* in Our image, according to Our likeness; let them have dominion over the fish of the sea, over the birds of the air, and over the cattle, over all the earth and over every creeping thing that creeps on the earth.' 27 So God created man in His *own* image; in the image of God He created him*; male and female He created them*. 28 Then God blessed them, and God said to them, 'Be fruitful and multiply; fill the earth and subdue it* ; have dominion over the fish of the sea, over the birds of the air, and over every living thing that moves on the earth.' 29 And God said, 'See, I have given you every herb *that* yields seed which *is* on the face of all the earth, and every tree whose fruit yields seed; to you it shall be for food. 30 Also, to every beast of the earth, to every bird of the air, and to everything that creeps on the earth, in which *there is* life, *I have given* every green herb for food'; and it was so. 31 Then God saw everything that He had made, and indeed *it was* very good. So the evening and the morning were the sixth day." Gen. 1:1-31

First He created* the heavens and the earth, in other words He called [He spoke into existence] the Physical structure of the universe [Cosmos] as a system of order and harmony. Next He created* every thing that moves or has life, the "Biological," or what is known as the science of plants and animals. Then He created* man in His image, male and female He created them. This creation was out of nothing or as a Spiritual component of creation, and then He made* man out of the dust of the ground as a physical part of creation. So man was both created* and then made*.

Man and woman alone are God's only Physical, Biological, and Spiritual beings created and made in the image of God. Mankind is the only component of God's creation able to have communication with Him, other than angels. All of God's other complex systems or components of creation were made by God, such as the Sun and Moon [Great lights]; the beasts of the fields, the cattle, and all that creeps on the earth. Notice: In Gen. 1;31, everything was "very good." God is still "creating" today.

16 "Therefore, from now on, we regard no one according to the flesh. Even though we have known Christ according to the flesh, yet now we know *Him thus* no longer. 17 Therefore, if anyone *is* in Christ, *he is* a new

creation; old things have passed away; behold, all things have become new." 2 Cor. 5:16,17

Another facet of God's revelation of His ways is to explore His repeated use of "Let." Why does He say "Let"? Perhaps in His mind His overall plan has steps and portions that require a timing to their release. It is as if He had stored away every component of His creation and He called forth their release by His "Let" command. This magnificent way of His making things is far from our knowing or understanding, but isn't it interesting to contemplate about these wonders of Our Father? Just give thought to the things He is drawing us into as His Family.

Does His revelation of His plans and ways give us a peek of what we, His children, will be doing with Him in Our future? There are other interesting words He speaks such as: "According to its kind," and "Concerning fruit, herbs, and trees whose seed is in itself." These statements eliminate all possibility of any "Evolution" of species.

What God <u>creates</u> lasts forever, what is <u>made</u> may disintegrate and die. This is the story about the Heart of Man, and the Heart of God, and HOW THEY COME TOGETHER. The Heart of God desired a loving family of children on which He may pour out His love, joy, and blessings, <u>but the children must be completely like Him in every respect</u>! He required His family to love Him and fulfill only His plans for them. This necessitated each member of His family to not only be in God's likeness and image, Gen. 1:26,27 on the outside, their external appearance, but He required their internal, their Spirit Self, to be in His Spiritual likeness and image.

Love freely returned must come from a love that is released freely and completely, so God had to set a plan to let His children go out on their own to choose Him or choose self. [This free will agent, self, was given by God to man] This pursuit through the Scriptures will concentrate only on Man's Heart in different times and through different ages seeking a clear path back to the Father, and on God's Heart as He saw man's walk. This book seeks, by a display of men's walk through life, to teach you what to look for that is pleasing to God. You <u>should not wish or hope</u> to please God <u>you should only learn to do it!</u> Try to be consistent in this pursuit, learn to catch the flow, the rhyme, and the rhythm of God's desires in your own daily life.

The involvement in God's plan of the fallen angels, and Lucifer, has never been completely explained. Here then is a brief background of how Satan got caught up in man's development. Sometime prior to or during creating the Heavens, the Earth and Man, God created an innumerable company of beings described as angels. [The Chumash, the "Stone Edition" 1995, says in their second day comments on Genesis, "on this day God was still the only spiritual being in existence, for the angels were not created until the second day"]

The Bible is quiet about the timing when the angels were created or what most of them looked like, but isn't it reasonable to think that any creation that exists and is meant to be close to God must be "God like." However they were created similar to what men would be like, they had personality, and were capable of great intelligence and moral responsibility. They apparently were created all at the same time and were all given eternal life, and they do not seem to increase in numbers through any method of birth. They seemed to be given their tasks by divine appointment, and they were also held responsible for the quality of their service and their moral choices. Generally angels fall in two categories: 1. The fallen angels, 2. The unfallen angels. Both groups of angels are to be discussed regarding their impact on mankind.

"In the beginning God created the heavens and the earth. The earth was without form and void: and darkness was on the face of the deep. And the Spirit of God was hovering over the face of the waters." Gen. 1:1,2

Men have raised many questions about these two verses, here is one story: In verses one and two it appears that God created earth, verse one, then He, in verse two, seems to have lost control, but that was not what happened. God gave release to "Lucifer the Son of the Morning" to do works on his own, and he [Lucifer] took great pleasure in thinking he was fashioning his kingdom, but he laid waste to what had to be reformed. God, knowing all that happens, used Lucifer's desires to set in motion a sequence of events that God would use to help make His family.

Now before the beginning of the heavens and earth, God had a great desire to have a family of children just like Him. As this desire was forming He knew He should supply them with a proper world to grow and form in, so He created the heavens and the earth. This work so intrigued the angels, that Lucifer, the Son of the Morning, [This was his name because he was created in the Morning of God's creation] decided to follow and observe God's handiwork, and then Lucifer had the forming of a plan to use the creation for his own purposes. He desired to be like God and form his own kingdom.

6 "To what were its foundations fastened? Or who laid its cornerstone, 7When the morning stars sang together, And all the sons of God shouted for joy." Job 38:6,7 [Note sons of God were the angels]
14"You *were* the anointed cherub who covers; I established you; You were on the holy mountain of God; You walked back and forth in the midst of fiery stones. 5You *were* perfect in your ways from the day you were created, till iniquity was found in you." Eze. 28:14,15

"You were perfect," this could mean that Lucifer was perfect for the task God created him for. Lucifer saw the earth forming and set himself to use it, God knew and gave reign to Lucifer's desires. Lucifer pulled a third of the lower angels with him and so contaminated God's beginning that he laid waste to that earth forming, and it required reforming. It is true that God released Lucifer to do works on his own, and Lucifer took great pleasure in thinking he was fashioning his kingdom, but this was the time of God exposing Lucifer's rebellion and casting him out of heaven. Man has, without God's prompting, carried this tale too far.

This also is a time of God changing his relationship with the angels; they, from this time [of Lucifer's rebellion], would not enjoy the closeness of God's company they had previously enjoyed. They lost their close walk and their previously allowed privileges. The angels would be in a position of servants and messengers of God and not in intimate relation with Him and or His plans. Men would be aware of the angel's separate walk because God allows Satan and some to his fallen angels to be used as a tool of work helping to select and give purpose to men's growth. At the end of man's growing time on earth, God will terminate Satan's usefulness and his army of uselessness! Note: This is the background to Eph. 3:10 which indicates that God would not allow the angelic rulers to understand some of the complicated aspects of God's many sided wisdom until it was shown to them through the church.

9 "and to make all see what *is* the fellowship of the mystery, which from the beginning of the ages has been hidden in God who created all things through Jesus Christ; 10 <u>to the intent that now the manifold wisdom of God might be made known by the church to the principalities and powers in the heavenly *places*,</u> 11 according to the eternal purpose which He accomplished in Christ Jesus our Lord." Eph. 3: 9-11

GOD'S PLAN BEGINS

Adam was set in the garden by the Father with minimum instructions to tend, guard and keep it.

15 "Then the LORD God took the man and put him in the garden of Eden to tend and keep it. 16 And the LORD God commanded the man, saying, 'Of every tree of the garden you may freely eat; 17 but of the tree of the knowledge of good and evil you shall not eat, for in the day that you eat of it you shall surely die.'" Gen. 2:15-17

God knowing there was a serpent [Satan the fallen angel] loose told Adam only to "guard" his garden, not from who or what. This set the stage for Adam to move freely on His own with only one caution:

2 "And the woman said to the serpent, 'We may eat the fruit of the trees of the garden; 3 but of the fruit of the tree which *is* in the midst of the garden, God has said, 'You shall not eat it, nor shall you touch it, lest you die.' " Gen.3: 2,3

This simple instruction was enough for Adam to fail, because in his heart he desired to please himself and go his own way not God's way. [Adam started man's stony heart] Adam and Eve could have repented and asked for forgiveness and God would have done that, but it was their finger pointing and lack of accepting blame that caused their downfall. How did the heart of man become so quickly polluted? To answer that question a look must be given to the situation in the Garden of Eden. God had prepared the garden so Adam would be completely supported with every need fulfilled. God is still like that today He has all of man's requirements set apart and available when man learns how to obey God's desire and not submit to man's self-pleasing.

God never warned Adam about the enemy hovering about Eden, other than by saying "guard" the garden. Understand if Adam had taken proper care of the garden then the whole earth was his to use. But to answer the question what polluted man's heart so quickly? Adam allowed self-pleasing to take first place instead of obeying God's command to not eat of the fruit of the tree of Good and Evil. This one act of disobedience gave Satan the opportunity to take possession of Adam and all God had given to him, the whole earth and all that was in it.

With Adam's disobedience, Satan's Angel of Death came upon mankind and fear was allowed to reign, thus putting every man born on earth in control of the Spirit of Fear "The Death Angel." The curse of "Fear" came to man along with the curse put upon the whole earth by God. This explains the quick fall of all men as God stated in Gen. 6:5-8. The flood of evil angels moving into and taking possession of the earth and all that was in it polluted man's heart. This "Fear Factor" is the basic reason for man's quick fall and his heart becoming polluted bringing on God's reason for the flood. God never removed this "Fear Factor" but He began a way to use it, and to help man to be set free of this sin through the Blood Sacrifice He instituted for the children of Israel years later. This was only a partial fix and it was with the sacrifice of Jesus on the cross that provided man's only sure way of having a pure heart and freedom from fear, but that's later on in the story.

This <u>heart failure</u> was the heart failure of man's human spirit. To make this heart story clear "The Heart" pursued in this book is man's "human spirit's heart" and this is the heart to be replaced by a new heart. So Adam's problem becomes one of man's ways of defeat, but what are man's ways of salvation, and how will he come to the Father? By skipping from one heart to another this book will show, through this progression, how the path God desires for men will open up, and how men will return into the Father's arms, [Their spirit came from Him in the first place]. It will also show man's path of separation from Him forever.

Scripture clearly reveals man's fall and his problems from the beginning. Who then did right, and was found pleasing to God, and how was that done? Who failed completely and was lost to God forever? Adam was the first man to sin and fall from God's grace, [He was the one God gave the commandment to] thus indicating one way that man will win or lose his place with God. Abel was the first man to be killed, this raised the necessity for God to provide a place of safe keeping for all those who were to be taken in death, for death reigned from Adam to Noah, and then on to Moses. Rom. 5:12-14.

As yet there were no places in Earth for Death, Hell, or Abraham's Bosom, and there were no places such as the Abyss and the chains of darkness for fallen angels. Here are some scriptures helping man to understand these places.

4 "For if God did not spare the angels who sinned, but cast *them* down to <u>hell</u> and delivered *them* into <u>chains of darkness, to</u> be reserved for judgment. . ." 11 Pet. 2:4

6 "And the angels who did not keep their proper domain, but left their own abode, He has reserved in <u>everlasting chains under darkness</u> for the judgment of the great day." Jude 6

48 "What man can live and not see <u>death</u>? Can he deliver from the power of the <u>grave</u>?" Ps 89:48

18 "I am He who lives, and was dead, and behold, I am alive forevermore Amen. And I have the keys of <u>Hades and Death</u>." Rev. 1;18

22 "So it was that the beggar died, and was carried by the Angels to <u>Abraham"s bosom</u>. The rich man also died and was buried." Lu. 16:22

God had to provide these hiding places because these men did not wholly belong to Him; they were Satan's because of the transfer of Earth to him by Adam's sin. [Note: Satan can't create and he certainly wouldn't be the one to make these future places of his own internment.] God had to secrete these men away in a holding place where they could later be rescued. He had no right to remove men from the earth until Jesus conquered Satan at his resurrection.

19 "· · ·by whom also He went and <u>preached to the spirits in prison</u>, 20 who formerly were disobedient, when once the Divine longsuffering

waited in the days of Noah, while *the* ark was being prepared, in which a few, that is, eight souls, were saved through water." 1 Pet 3:19,20

This scripture is speaking about Jesus when He went into one of these places, and what He preached has not been made known to anyone except to those spirits in that prison, the people of Adam's time. Anyone created by the breath of God was an eternal being, this fact required God to provide for each ones eternal place in the Universe. [Wherever men's heart would lead them.] It followed then that God put all men from Adam to the flood in a place in the Earth after their death. But Death reigned from Adam to Moses, even over all those who did not transgress as Adam had; they also had to have a place to wait. So God created Death, Hell, and later Abraham's Bosom, all places in the Earth to be used until Jesus would free them or transfer them to an eternal place of their own choosing.

DEATH: Death as a place was not God's desire, but only God's provision for a time. Death was a necessary place of abode, a place of waiting, holding and hiding. Some things should be made clear about that place. It was a safe place for God's children, and there are several areas for separate groups of men. Satan was overall temporary owner, but he did not have complete power because he was still watched over by the Father in everything he did. Here are some scriptures concerning death:

10"Who can count the dust of Jacob,   Or number one-fourth of Israel? Let me die the <u>death of the righteous</u>, And let my end be like his!" Num. 23:10

5 "For in death *there is* no remembrance of You; In the grave who will give You thanks?" Ps 6:5

20 "Our God *is* the God of salvation; And to GOD the Lord *belong* escapes from death.." Ps. 68:20

15 "Precious in the sight of the LORD *Is* the death of His saints." Ps.116:15

36 "But he who sins against me wrongs his own soul; All those who hate me love death." Prov. 8:36

21 "Death and life *are* in the power of the tongue, And those who love it will eat its fruit." Prov. 18:21 8 "He will swallow up death forever, And

the Lord GOD will wipe away tears from all faces; The rebuke of His people He will take away from all the earth; For the LORD has spoken." Isa. 25:8

28 "Assuredly, I say to you, there are some standing here who shall not taste death till they see the Son of Man coming in His kingdom." Matt. 16:28

24 " Most assuredly, I say to you, he who hears My word and believes in Him who sent Me has everlasting life, and shall not come into judgment, but has passed from death into life." John 5:24

52 "Then the Jews said to Him, "Now we know that You have a demon! Abraham is dead, and the prophets; and You say, If anyone keeps My word he shall never taste death." John 8:52

It is important to review these scriptures:

12 "Therefore, just as through one man sin entered the world, and death through sin, and thus death spread to all men, because all sinned— 13 (For until the law sin was in the world, but sin is not imputed when there is no law. 14 Nevertheless death reigned from Adam to Moses, _even over those who had not sinned_ according to the likeness of the transgression of Adam, who is a type of Him who was to come." Rom. 5;12-14

Therefore as sin came into the world through one man, and death as the result of sin, so death spread to all men, no one being able to stop it or escape its power, because all men sinned. To be sure sin was in the world before even the law was given, but sin is not charged to men's account where there is no law [to transgress]. Yet death held sway from Adam to Moses, [the law giver] even over those who did not themselves transgress [a positive command] as Adam had. Adam was a type [prefigure] of the One Who was to come. [In reverse, the former destructive, the later saving.]

Concerning born again Christians they have been set free from sin and death.

5 "For if we have been united together in the likeness of His death, certainly we also shall be *in the likeness* of *His* resurrection, 6 knowing this,

that <u>our old man was crucified with *Him*,</u> that the body of sin might be done away with, that we should no longer be slaves of sin. [7] For he who has died has been freed from sin. [8] Now if we died with Christ, we believe that we shall also live with Him, [9] knowing that Christ, having been raised from the dead, dies no more. Death no longer has dominion over Him. [10] For *the death* that He died, He died to sin once for all; but *the life* that He lives, He lives to God. [11] Likewise you also, <u>reckon your-selves to be dead indeed to sin,</u> but alive to God in Christ Jesus our Lord." Rom. 6:5-11

[2] "For the law of the Spirit of life in Christ Jesus <u>has made me free from the law of sin and death</u>." Rom. 8:2

Through one man death came, also through one man came resurrection of the dead.

[20] "But now Christ is risen from the dead, *and* has become the first fruits of those who have fallen asleep. [21] For since by man *came* death, by Man also *came* the resurrection of the dead. [22] For as in Adam all die, even so in Christ <u>all shall be made alive."</u> 1 Cor. 15:20-22

Jesus experienced death for everyone.

[9] "But we see Jesus, who was made a little lower than the angels, for the suffering of death crowned with glory and honor, that He, <u>by the grace of God, might taste death for everyone</u>." Heb. 2:9

Jesus took the keys to death and Hell.

[17] "And when I saw Him, I fell at His feet as dead. But He laid His right hand on me, saying to me, 'Do not be afraid, I am the first and the last.

[18] I am He who lives, and was dead, and behold, I am alive forevermore. Amen. <u>And I have the keys of Hades and of Death</u>.'" Rev. 1:17,18

This is a brief overall picture of death as it occurs during the span of the life of man. Now take a look at the other places in the earth that God provided.

HADES [HELL, SHEOL] AND CHAINS IN DARKNESS

"I am He who lives, and was dead, and behold, I am alive forevermore. Amen. And I have the keys of <u>Hades and of Death</u>." Rev. 1:18 The works men do lives after them, and evil produced has to be given expression, but I [God] must contain the evil of men and angels. The place-ment of evil is man's doing by My release of man's will. This expression must be held in a place of My choosing, so I have given a prison in earth for the control of evil expression. This will later be disposed of forever as useless expressions contained, for the future safety of My plans. I have set places in earth as control areas of necessity. The death place [Part of hell] for man is such an area; Hades [Another part of hell] is the worst part of that prison. No useful purpose is served by exploring the evil of man's losses. My release of self-serving, both in man and angels, has shown the necessity of control by use of positive containment.

4 "For certain men have crept in unnoticed, who long ago were marked out for this condemnation, ungodly men, who turn the grace of our God into lewdness and deny the only Lord God and our Lord Jesus Christ. 5 But I want to remind you, though you once knew this, that the Lord, having saved the people out of the land of Egypt, afterward destroyed those who did not believe. 6 And the angels who did not keep their proper domain, but left their own abode, He has reserved in <u>everlasting chains under darkness for the judgment of the great day</u>; 7 as Sodom and Gomorrah, and the cities around them in a similar manner to these, having given themselves over to sexual immorality and gone after strange flesh, are set forth as an example, suffering the vengeance of eternal fire. But you, beloved, building yourselves up on your most holy faith, praying in the Holy Spirit." 21 "Keep yourselves in the love of God, looking for the mercy of our Lord Jesus Christ unto eternal life. 22 And on some have compassion, making a distinction; 23 but others save with fear, pulling *them* out of the fire, hating even the garment defiled by the flesh." Jude 4-7 and 20-23

PAUSE AND REFLECT

THE ABOVE CHAPTER SETS THE SCENE FOR GOD'S RECOVERY OF LOST MAN. HOW GOD'S HEART WAS PAINED AT THE TURN OF MAN'S HEART FROM GOD LOVING TO SELF-LOVING. GOD HAD TO BUILD A METHOD SO HE COULD LEGALLY ENTER EARTH THAT NOW BELONGED TO SATAN. SATAN'S WICKEDNESS WAS FREE TO PERMEATE THE CHILDREN OF GOD. DEATH REIGNED OVER MEN BRINGING ITS PRODUCT, FEAR. ALL MEN WERE UNDER THREAT OF DEATH, AS FEAR WAS THEIR TORMENTOR. AS GOD SLOWLY MOVED ON SOME MEN'S HEARTS, DRAWING THEM INTO A PATH OF HIS LOVE, MOST MEN WERE LOST TO FEAR AND TORMENT, CAUSING THEIR SELF TO SEEK DOMINANCE THROUGH THEIR OWN STRENGTH. SATAN OWNED THE EARTH AND ALL THAT WAS IN IT AND FEAR GAVE HIM CONTROL OVER MAN. UNDER SATAN, SIN AND EVIL REIGNED, AND HE DESIRED TO KEEP FULL AUTHORITY OVER MAN.

THIS BEGINNING CAN GIVE VIEW TO HOW GOD DESIRED TO DRAW MAN BACK INTO HIS ORIGINAL PLACE. HE WAS TO HAVE CONTROL AND AUTHORITY OVER THE WHOLE EARTH. HE WAS TO MAKE IT LIKE THE GARDEN OF EDEN. THE WHOLE EARTH WAS TO BE MADE LIKE HEAVEN ON EARTH. GOD'S PLAN HAS NEVER CHANGED NO MATTER WHAT ADAM AND EVE DID. THEIR TRANSGRESSION HAS SET A NEW COURSE FOR MAN WHICH IS DIFFERENT THAN GOD'S FIRST PLAN. MAN STARTED OUT PERFECT LIKE GOD IN ALL HIS WAYS, BUT FAILURE DERAILED THAT APPROACH. GOD'S SECOND PLAN WAS CLEARLY CHANGED BECAUSE MAN HAD TO BE RESCUED FROM SATAN'S CONTROL. SO ON REFLECTION ONE CAN SEE THE REARRANGED PLAN OF GOD NOW TAKING PLACE.

CHAPTER TWO

MEN WORK GOD'S PLAN

Adam's heart is exposed by his actions. He was standing by when the serpent was enticing Eve, and He went along with all that was being said to her. As Eve had sinned by self-pleasing, so God condemned Adam for disobeying Him, listening to his wife, and eating what she had given to him. Adam blamed his wife, Eve blamed the serpent, and both of them refused to take any blame.

17 Then to Adam He said, "Because you have heeded the voice of your wife, and have eaten from the tree of which I commanded you, saying, 'You shall not eat of it': Cursed *is* the ground for your sake; In toil you shall eat *of* it all the days of your life." Gen. 3:17

WHAT WAS ADAM'S HEART FAILURE? *

He disobeyed what God had said to him. [God said do not——] He heard the Serpent doubt God's word, and he gave heed to the lies because it sounded pleasing to him. It was his desire to be wise, he saw things pleasing to him that looked good, and he wanted to know the difference between good and evil. What then was his error, *<u>he desired to please self not God;</u> also he failed to seek God's help or ask for forgiveness.

Perhaps another observance of the Adam and Eve presented in the Bible would have to be one of loving forgiveness, because he and Eve had been given Spirits that could communicate with God, but they didn't have that much time to grow to know God's love or His purposes. God's instructions had been for them to tend the garden and guard it! They apparently had never had time to know God the Father and His loving ways well enough to understand God's plan or desires for them. Everything was new to them and there was so much to see and do that the wonder of their garden overwhelmed them, they had nothing else with which to compare their situation.

If they had stopped to consider everything in Eden had been given to them except "The Tree;" then they may have figured out that that one tree was God's, it didn't belong to them! But there never had been anything said about sin or stealing and they were still very intrigued with their whole garden. What if Adam had just tended all the trees as he was asked to do, but he gave special attention to God's "Tree" out of love for God. What if Adam had, after lovingly caring for God's "Tree," had picked the fruit from it and made it a gift to God when they had their afternoon walk together in the garden. Don't you imagine God would be so moved in His heart, seeing this loving gesture that He would give Adam further explanations of Good and Evil? Don't you believe God, as a loving Father, would explain, through time, the whole story of the "Good and Evil Tree"? If Adam or Eve had only loved God and His desires more than their desires; but where would that leave all of us? Didn't Our Loving Heavenly Father really know all that would happen and isn't it working out beautifully for all of His Children?

WHAT WAS CAIN'S HEART FAILURE? *

At the time for bringing offerings to the Lord, Cain and Abel both gave gifts to the Lord, Cain gave his gift from the field and Abel gave a gift from his flocks.

3 "And in the process of time it came to pass that Cain brought an offering of the fruit of the ground to the LORD. 4 Abel also brought of the firstborn of his flock and of their fat. And the LORD respected Abel and his offering, 5 but He did not respect Cain and his offering. And Cain was very angry, and his countenance fell. 6 So the LORD said to Cain, "Why are you angry? And why has your countenance fallen? 7 If you do well, will you not be accepted? And if you do not do well, sin lies at the door. And its desire *is* for you, but you should rule over it." 8 Now Cain talked with Abel his brother; and it came to pass, when they were in the field, that Cain rose up against Abel his brother and killed him." Gen. 4:3-8

God gave Cain no respect or regard concerning his offering. Cain did not properly consider his gift, which was fruit from cursed ground; therefore, his gift was improper. Cain was self-pleasing not God pleasing, he became sad, depressed, angry and indignant. God said he could be accepted if he did well, but sin was at his door, and he needed to conquer it. He didn't conquer it; he proceeded to kill his brother. How had Cain failed? *His pride was hurt, and he sought revenge allowing the evil one to motivate him.

11 "For this is the message that you heard from the beginning, that we should love one another, 12 not as Cain *who* was of the wicked one and murdered his brother. And why did he murder him? Because his works were evil and his brother's righteous." 1 John 3:11,12

WHAT WAS ENOCH'S HEART LIKE? *

Cain left the presence of God got married and had a son named Enoch. Enoch married and had sons. It was said of him that *he pleased God and he walked with God.

16 "Then Cain went out from the presence of the LORD and dwelt in the land of Nod on the east of Eden. 17 And Cain knew his wife, and she conceived and bore Enoch. And he built a city, and called the name of the city

after the name of his son—Enoch. ^{18} To Enoch was born Irad; and Irad begot Mehujael, and Mehujael begot Methushael, and Methushael begot Lamech." Gen. 4:16-18

Enoch at birth was blessed of the Lord; his Father Cain built a city naming it after Enoch his son. God further blessed Enoch by blessing his children; God gave his offspring prominent places in the growing population of the earth. Jabal become the father of all those who dwelled in tents and had cattle and possessions. There were musicians such as Jubal who played the lyre and pipe. Tubal-Cain became a worker of bronze and iron, and then there was Methuselah to whom God gave the longest life known to man, nine hundred and sixty-nine years.

^{14} "Now Enoch, the seventh from Adam, prophesied about these men also, saying, 'Behold, the Lord comes with ten thousands of His saints, ^{15} to execute judgment on all, to convict all who are ungodly among them of all their ungodly deeds which they have committed in an ungodly way, and of all the harsh things which ungodly sinners have spoken against Him.'" Jude 14,15

^{37} ". . .the son of Methuselah, *the son* of Enoch, *the son* of Jared, *the son* of Mahalalel, *the son* of Cainan, ^{38} the son of Enosh, *the son* of Seth, *the son* of Adam, *the son* of God." Luke 3:37,38

^{5} "By faith <u>Enoch was taken away</u> so that he did not see death, *'and was not found, because God had taken him'*; for before he was taken he had this testimony, that he pleased God. ^{6} But without faith *it is* impossible to please *Him*, for he who comes to God must believe that He is, and *that* He is a rewarder of those who diligently seek Him." Heb. 11: 5, 6

"Enoch was taken away," [translated] this is an instant that seems to indicate God had a place in the earth for the men He loved. God couldn't take them from the earth because they belonged to Satan. Hebrews 11:5,6 says without faith it is impossible to please God, and God is a rewarder of those who diligently seek Him. These scriptures seems to give theory to the fact that God created a "Heaven in the earth" because Enoch was taken, transferred, or translated according to the King James Bible, but the Amplified Bible says "Caught up" and then says transferred to heaven. Now John 3:13 says [Jesus speaking], "No one has ascended to heaven but He who came down from heaven, that is, the Son of Man who is in heaven."

The truth of these statements seems clear: God made a "heaven like" place in the earth for those who pleased Him. Elijah had a similar experience [2 Kings 2:1,11] he was caught up in the air and then he must have entered into the earth into God's prepared place, out of sight of man. Moses was also taken and men knew not where he went, or was buried, however Moses and Elijah both appeared with Jesus on earth at His transfiguration [Mk 9:2-7], it seems as if they both were hanging around earth. All of these scriptures raise questions, but it would seem they are simply answered by a "heaven in earth" where God kept His loved ones until Jesus could draw "Abraham's Bosom", [isn't this a heaven in the earth called Paradise?] with Him into heaven at His ascent. At Jesus' ascent was the first time men were taken to heaven.

7 "But to each one of us grace was given according to the measure of Christ's gift. 8 Therefore He says: '_When He ascended on high, He led captivity captive, And gave gifts to men._' 9 (Now this, _"He ascended"_— what does it mean but that He also first descended into the lower parts of the earth? 10 He who descended is also the One who ascended far above all the heavens, that He might fill all things.)" Eph. 4:7-10

If that wasn't enough of God blessing Enoch, Noah was a direct descendent from Enoch. In Jude 14 it States " Enoch was a prophet of God and born in the seventh generation from Adam. Heb. 11:5 says Enoch had great faith, enough that God transferred him to Heaven, and there was testimony that Enoch pleased and had been a satisfaction to God. So it must be said *Enoch's heart was right with God, Luke 3:37,38 states Enoch was in direct linage of Jesus. To know Enoch's heart his ways must be followed. He gave more attention to the things the Father was talking to him about than what the world around him was interested in. His time was given over to time spent in quiet places with God, and he did not stop his ears to God talking. Everyone captures God's attention by setting himself apart from man, and turning his time and attention to the Father. This worked in the very beginning when God walked with Adam in the cool of the day, and it works today, God being the same, yesterday, today, and forever.

[7] "Remember those who rule over you, who have spoken the word of God to you, whose faith follow, considering the outcome of *their* conduct. [8] Jesus Christ *is* the same yesterday, today, and forever. [9] Do not be carried about with various and strange doctrines. <u>For *it is* good that the heart be established by grace,</u> not with foods which have not profited those who have been occupied with them." Heb. 13:7-9

WHAT WAS NOAH'S HEART LIKE? *

As men began to multiply on the face of the land God saw the wickedness of man was great on the earth, but Noah found grace [favor] in the eyes of the Lord.

[3] "And the LORD said, 'My Spirit shall not strive with man forever, for he *is* indeed flesh; yet his days shall be one hundred and twenty years.' [4] There were giants on the earth in those days, and also afterward, when <u>the sons of God came in to the daughters of men</u> and they bore *children* to them. Those *were* the mighty men who *were* of old, men of renown. Now it came to pass, when men began to multiply on the face of the earth, and daughters were born to them, . . .that the sons of God saw the daughters of men, that they *were* beautiful; and they took wives for themselves of all whom they chose. [5] Then the LORD saw that the wickedness of man *was* great in the earth, and *that* <u>every intent of the thoughts of his heart *was* only evil continually</u>. [6] And the LORD was sorry that He had made man on the earth, and He was <u>grieved in His heart</u>. [7] So the LORD said, 'I will destroy man whom I have created from the face of the earth, both man and beast, creeping thing and birds of the air, for I am sorry that I have made them.' [8] But <u>Noah found grace</u> in the eyes of the LORD. [9] This is the genealogy of Noah. Noah was a just man, perfect in his generations. Noah walked with God." Gen.6:3-9   Noah was just, righteous, and blameless in an evil generation.

Then the LORD said to Noah, "Come into the ark, you and all your household, because I have <u>seen *that* you *are* righteous</u> before Me in this generation." Gen. 7:1

He walked in habitual fellowship with God, Gen. 6:9, he did all that God commanded him. As Enoch had warned the people about God, Jude 14,15, so also had Noah, he preached righteousness to them.

5 ". . .and did not spare the ancient world, but saved Noah, *one of* eight *people,* a preacher of righteousness, bringing in the flood on the world of the ungodly. . ." II Pet. 2:5

After the flood, and the ark was emptied, God pronounced a blessing upon Noah and his sons telling them to be fruitful and multiply.

So God blessed Noah and his sons, and said to them: "Be fruitful and multiply, and fill the earth." Gen. 9:1

Therefore Noah's *heart proved right before God* by his consistent actions of obedience and love for the things of God. My love goes out to all of My children, especially those in the Adam to Noah's time. They were all put in difficult and dangerous situations without much guidance or coverage. Their times were finally overwhelmed by Satan's evil and this brought My wrath. To have the loving devoted ones, which came through those times, was a great blessing to Me, and I have a place of high regard for the successful men and women of that time. Their example has never been given enough attention and this book calls for all My children to stop and give thought to the loving action from them that brought them to a place of love in My heart.

Surely they were men and women with much longer lives and therefore they each one had a great time span to search their hearts to find My way for them, very few were able to take advantage of their opportunities. Noah proved a most consistent companion to Me and proved his loyalty time and time again. His consistent attention to the things I desired was a hall mark of great importance to continuing of man's race. Enoch was a man of remarkable love and he maintained contact with Me daily, this was a wonderful effort, which I could never overlook. Yes there were many who took advantage of their long lives and I found a close walk was possible with many children of that time.

All are carefully watched over in My place of safety in the earth until their time of rescue and release occurs. What great times are just ahead for Jesus' church, and then all the earth's loved ones will have their final release. They will come into their last chapter of growth during the 1000 years just ahead. It is interesting to note I make very little of Adam after his fall. He pursued no special love for Me and carried on in his pursuit of self and self's purposes. My heart goes out to all of My children, but they all have their place with Me or without Me, it has been their choice by their actions and desires to make their ways unchangeable.

COMMENT ON THE FIRST MAN*
All of life is about God choosing man and man choosing God.

God's choice was made clear in the beginning, when God chose to make a family. The family of God was to be all, each and every one, just like Jesus.

34 "Jesus answered them, ' Is it not written in your law, I said, "You are Gods'? 35 If He called them gods, to whom the word of God came [and scripture cannot be broken], 36 do you say of Him whom the Father sanctified and sent into the world, You are blaspheming, because I said, I am the Son of God?" John 10:34-36

6 "I said, 'You *are* gods, and all of you are children of the Most High.'" Ps 82:6

What else could God's word mean?

26 "Then God said, 'Let Us make man in Our image, according to Our likeness; let them have dominion over the fish of the sea, over the birds of the air, and over the cattle, over all the earth and over every creeping thing that creeps on the earth.' 27 So God created man in His *own* image; in the image of God He created him; male and female He created them." Gen. 1:26,27

The **First Man** was God's beginning of His family, but God did not fully instruct or equip the first man for all that life and living was going to bring to him. God blessed them and said be fruitful and multiply and fill the earth etc. Gen. 1:28-30. God's plan had a deeper and concealed purpose for his family. It was that no family member should come to Him except out of love for God. God is love, God is light, and only children of His love and light would be proper family throughout eternity. God's long view was to require testing of man for selection to eternal life.

God's **FIRST MAN** Adam was set up to start man's life on earth, and is the beginning of the forming of God's family. As has been shown, man was overcome by Satan, Sin, and Self, then God, instead of giving men up at the time of the flood, saved only eight persons of Noah's family, and He used them to start again the forming of His Eternal Family.

Perhaps God's plan was from before the beginning of His creation of angels, heavens, and earth. God was to have a Family that would be just like Him and would love Him without reservation. This meant everyone in His family must be tested and proven to come to Him only out of love for Him. All candidates for eternal life must be given the choice of life and good, or death and evil!

15 "See, I have set before you today life and good, death and evil, 16 in that I command you today to love the LORD your God, to walk in His ways, and to keep His commandments, His statutes, and His judgments, that you may live and multiply; and the LORD your God will bless you in the land which you go to possess. 17 But if your heart turns away so that you do not hear, and are drawn away, and worship other gods and serve them, 18 I announce to you today that you shall surely perish; you shall not prolong *your* days in the land which you cross over the Jordan to go in and possess. 19 I call heaven and earth as witnesses today against you, *that* I have set before you life and death, blessing and cursing; therefore choose life, that both you and your descendants may live. . ." Deut. 30:15-19

This separation would be determined by their love of God or their love of self. The **FIRST MAN** *choosing was Adam, he was God's beginning in the forming of His physical [earth] family, which was necessary before He created His Heavenly Spiritual Family. This book is just picking the highlights of how God has been working His plan. Man is the crowning work of God, and His desire for His family was formed in His heart of love from before creation of Angels, Heavens and Earth. Angels were created beings used by God for filling His need for Messengers, ministers and servants, to occupy the place of support for His Family to be. * God entered man this first time only by breathing His breath into man, <u>God rising</u> through His breath only!

God's **"FIRST MAN"** period brought God's plan along to the time and place where God would then have a requirement for God's **"FIRST FAMILY"** forming along with God's law being given. Man was to be tested against God's requirements for His family, so the law of God was to be set before the first family group.

PAUSE AND REFLECT

GOD WAS APPARENTLY TAKING STEPS, WELL CALCULATED, TO BRING MAN OUT OF SATAN'S GRASP AND INTO GOD'S FAMILY. THE RECAPTURING OF THE EARTH WOULD ALSO OCCUR ALONG WITH THE SLOW TESTING OF MAN IN THE EARTH'S EVIL ENVIRONMENT. MAN MUST LEARN TO OVERCOME SATAN, SIN, AND SELF, AND GOD WAS DETERMINED TO SET HIS PLAN TO DO JUST THAT. ALL DURING THIS TIME OF MAN'S RETURN TO GOD, FROM WHENCE HE CAME, MAN WOULD BE TESTED AND TRIED TO PROVE HIS ACCEPTABILITY IN GOD'S KINGDOM. THIS FIRST PERIOD SHOWS GOD'S DEEP CONCERN FOR THE HEART OF MAN. A CARE THAT SHALL NEVER END!

CHAPTER THREE

2000 YEARS ABRAHAM TO JESUS
THE HEART OF MAN EXPOSED
GOD HOVERING OVER ISRAEL
THE FIRST FAMILY CHOOSING

THIS CHAPTER CENTERS ON GOD PICKING A NATION [HIS FIRST FAMILY] FOR HIM TO BRING HIS LAW, AND BEGIN HIS PLAN TO RESCUE LOST MAN FROM HIMSELF AND SATAN'S HOLD ON MAN.

ABRAHAM, A DIFFERENT SORT.*

When analyzing men and their walk with God, the common view being used has been, "What was their <u>attitude</u> toward God," but surely with Abraham the <u>attitude</u> of God comes to the forefront. It is never said in the Word Abraham loved, sought after, searched for or made a great effort to find God.

17 "And the LORD said, 'Shall I hide from Abraham what I am doing, 18 since Abraham shall surely become a great and mighty nation, and all the nations of the earth shall be blessed in him? 19 <u>For I have known him</u>, in order that he may command his children and his household after him, that they keep the way of the LORD, to do righteousness and justice, that the LORD may bring to Abraham what He has spoken to him.'" Gen. 18:17-19

In Gen. 18:19 [Amplified Bible] God says, "For I have known [chosen, acknowledged] him, as My own, so that he may teach and command his children and the sons of his house after him to keep the way of the Lord, and to do what is just and righteous, so that the Lord may bring Abraham what he has promised him." God didn't tell Abram to leave UR of Chaldees, but He must have moved on Terah, Abram's father, causing him to take his close family west to Haram."

31 "And Terah took his son Abram and his grandson Lot, the son of Haran, and his daughter-in-law Sarai, his son Abram's wife, and they went out with them from Ur of the Chaldeans to go to the land of Canaan; and they came to Haran and dwelt there." Gen. 11:31

In Haran the Lord spoke to Abram, this is the first communication between God and Abram, telling him to go away for yourself, your own advantage, from your country. Now generally this book has looked into man's relation with God questioning why God blessed and loved each of the men written about. Abram doesn't fit the previous pattern that has been noted. It was God taking the initiative, choosing and moving into Abram's life, and then taking Abram on his journey to greatness with the Lord. In Abram's behalf he was always listening, and obeying all that the Lord told him. Abram's heart was proven right with God, but not as previous men or as the many that followed him. It might be said Abram was unique among men, so Abram departed as the Lord had directed him; Lot his nephew went with him.

Now the LORD had said to Abram: "'Get out of your country, From your family And from your father's house, To a land that I will show you. 2 I will make you a great nation; I will bless you And make your name great; And you shall be a blessing. 3 I will bless those who bless you, And I will curse him who curses you; And in you all the families of the earth shall be blessed." So Abram departed as the Lord had spoken to him. And Abram was seventy-five years old when he departed from Haran.'" Gen. 12:1-4

Abraham was a man I knew before his physical birth and one I especially raised for My special purpose. Through him I picked My selected nation to be formed, and through him I brought into earth, and into action,

My recovery plan for all of the children of the earth. Through Abraham's seed My Son, My only begotten Son, was to be returned to His place of forever after accomplishing Our planned salvation for My Heavenly Family. Abram, My Abraham, was always <u>on My heart</u> as a key element of My family gathering, and after Noah, Abraham was essential to Our plans. As to <u>Abraham's heart, I made it right and acceptable</u> from the beginning and he never disappointed Me through his trials and blessings. *

ISAAC, JACOB, AND JOSEPH: DID THEIR HEARTS DRAW THEM TO GOD?*

It is difficult to find any of these men calling out to God out of their love for Him, or even speaking of their love for Him, but they all were watched over by the Lord, and He guarded, guided, and protected them. Through these men Abraham's covenant was carried on. These men walked with God and God spoke to them, however it seems it was their birthright that kept them under God's constant care. They all prayed to God and obeyed God so their heart was acceptable to God.* It is obvious that God kept these men in His plan, but not obvious that there can be anything learned about their walk with God to aid the seeker who wants to know how to draw closer to the Father. The best lesson from these three men is to always be obedient <u>by listening and being led by God's Holy Spirit</u>! *

MOSES

This time is a very important event for God because He was using the family Abraham started to cause a testing and choosing period that would set a stage for forming God's first family of children. The Father took the 430 years in Egypt as an earth womb of birthing for His first wife.

40 "Now the sojourn of the children of Israel who lived in Egypt *was* four hundred and thirty years. 41 And it came to pass at the end of the four hundred and thirty years—<u>on that very same day</u>—it came to pass that all the armies of the LORD went out from the land of Egypt." Exo. 12:40-41

8 "'When I passed by you again and looked upon you, indeed your time *was* the time of love; so I spread My wing over you and covered your nakedness. Yes, I swore an oath to you and entered into a covenant with you, <u>and you became Mine</u>,' says the Lord God.'" Eze. 16:8

This first selection of people would have to be tough, hardy, and resilient; therefore they were put through a toughening and hardening process while they increased in their numbers. This brought His people to the period that God felt they were ready for Him to call them out. Then there was to be an occasion of great climaxes, a time for God to show all men His power, and for God to claim for Himself a people! A couple of weeks before God moved Israel out of Egypt He told them to begin a calendar of years, months, weeks, and days.

Now the LORD spoke to Moses and Aaron in the land of Egypt, saying, 2 "This month *shall be* your beginning of months; it *shall be* the first month of the year to you." Exo.12:1,2

This made <u>Israel the only nation on earth that had their own calendar</u>, which they maintain to this present time! He put them on notice that they were a unique gathering of people, and they were under God's own timetable. Such a thing had never happened before! Israel was given a preview of their Savior to be by the miracle of the "Passover" and the Feast of the Unleavened Bread. The children of Israel were given great wealth and health.

"And the LORD said to Moses, 'I will bring one more plague on Pharaoh and on Egypt. Afterward he will let you go from here. When he lets *you* go, he will surely drive you out of here altogether. 2 Speak now in the hearing of the people, and let every man ask from his neighbor and every woman from her neighbor, articles of silver and articles of gold.' 3 And the LORD gave the people favor in the sight of the Egyptians. Moreover the man Moses *was* very great in the land of Egypt, in the sight of Pharaoh's servants and in the sight of the people." Exo. 11:1-3

35 "Now the children of Israel had done according to the word of Moses, and they had asked from the Egyptians articles of silver, articles of gold,

and clothing. [36] And the LORD had given the people favor in the sight of the Egyptians, so that they granted them *what they requested."* Thus. Exo.12:35,36,37 He also brought them out with silver and gold, and they plundered the Egyptian there was none feeble among His tribes. Ps. 105:37

On the very last day of the 430 years God moved His people out of Egypt and none were sick, weak, or crippled! Moses was led of the Lord to take the children into the wilderness and not into Canaan, which was only an eleven-day journey. Thus the children of Israel embarked upon their God planned path to their promised land. They went through wildernesses, deserts, pits, draughts, and shadows of death. God had a planned purpose. [4] "Yet I *am* the LORD your God Ever since the land of Egypt, And you shall know no God but Me; For *there is* no savior besides Me. [5] I knew you in the wilderness, in the land of great drought." Hos. 13;4,5

So Moses brought Israel from the Red Sea, to Shur, Marah, Elim, and the Sinai. The Law was given at Sinai.

And God spoke all these words, saying: [2] "I *am* the LORD your God, who brought you out of the land of Egypt, out of the house of bondage. [3] You shall have no other gods before Me. [4] You shall not make for yourself a carved image—any likeness *of anything* that *is* in heaven above, or that *is* in the earth beneath, or that *is* in the water under the earth; [5] you shall not bow down to them nor serve them. For I, the LORD your God, *am* a jealous God, visiting the iniquity of the fathers upon the children to the third and fourth *generations* of those who hate Me, [6] but showing mercy to thousands, to those who love Me and keep My commandments. [7] You shall not take the name of the LORD your God in vain, for the LORD will not hold *him* guiltless who takes His name in vain. [8] Remember the Sabbath day, to keep it holy. [9] Six days you shall labor and do all your work, [10] but the seventh day *is* the Sabbath of the LORD your God. *In it* you shall do no work: you, nor your son, nor your daughter, nor your male servant, nor your female servant, nor your cattle, nor your stranger who *is* within your gates. [11] For *in* six days the LORD made the heavens and the earth, the sea, and all that *is* in them, and rested the seventh day. Therefore the LORD blessed the Sabbath day and hallowed it. [12] Honor your father and your mother, that your days may be long upon the land which the LORD your God is giving you. [13]You shall not murder [14] You shall not commit adultery. [15] You shall not steal. [16]You shall not bear false witness against your neighbor. [17] You shall not covet your neighbor's house; you shall not covet your neighbor's wife, nor his male servant, nor his female servant, nor his ox, nor his donkey, nor anything that *is* your neighbor's." Exo.20:1-17

Their journey then took Israel to the mountains of the Amorites where God set the promised land before them. Moses took them from Param and sent men to spy out the land of Canaan for 40 days where they saw the land, the people, cities, and fruit of the land and brought back an evil report. With only two spies giving a good report, God's anger was kindled against Israel and He made them wander 40 years in the wilderness, 40 years, a year for each day they were in the land spying.

[24] "Then they despised the pleasant land; They did not believe His word,
[25] But complained in their tents, *And* did not heed the voice of the LORD.
[26] Therefore He raised His hand *in an oath* against them, To overthrow them in the wilderness." Ps. 106:24-26

Moses led the children of Israel the 40 years, then brought them to the Jordan river. Then Moses went and spoke these words to all Israel.
[2] "And he said to them: 'I *am* one hundred and twenty years old today. I can no longer go out and come in. Also the LORD has said to me, 'You shall not cross over this Jordan.' [3] The LORD your God Himself crosses over before you; He will destroy these nations from before you, and you shall dispossess them. Joshua himself crosses over before you, just as the LORD has said. Deut. 31:1-3 [4] Then the LORD said to him, "This *is* the land of which I swore to give Abraham, Isaac, and Jacob, saying, 'I will give it to your descendants.' I have caused you to see *it* with your eyes, but you shall not cross over there.'"

5 So Moses the servant of the Lord died there in the land of Moab, according to the word of the Lord. Deut." 34:4,5

MOSES' HEART

God watched over Moses from before his birth, for God saw to it that Moses was born out of the loins of the House of Levi, and He made the child beautiful. God saw Moses raised as a king's son, and he was schooled properly for leadership. When the children of Israel cried out to God, God heard and He answered their cries. God appeared to Moses out of a burning brush only for one reason, He wanted to fully capture his attention. God caught his eye by the sight of the flames burning the bush. He caught the sense of his smell from the fumes of the burning, he caught Moses sense of feeling by the heat of burning, and finally God caught the ear of Moses by the sound of burning and the voice of God, and the taste of the burning was in the air. All of Moses' senses were captured; it was in this that God introduced Himself to Moses and this relationship continued in a way different than God has ever done with any one else.

Moses' task was greater and more difficult than the work required by any other man. God created a nation Israel as His first family through Moses, and He called them His first Wife. He set the scene of man's salvation in the awareness of man's conscious through the pass-over experience, and by the acts of miracles He worked through Moses. Moses was just a man, and he had a most difficult walk with the pressures of leadership imposed on him. His life was not like any other child of God has had. Moses had his failures and his triumphs. Moses was unique among men, and <u>his heart was special to God</u>, no one before Moses spent so much time alone with the Lord, or wrote down as much as the Lord commanded him to record. [Unless it was Noah, who was counseled by God for 100 years during the building of the Arc]

27 "Then the LORD said to Moses, 'Write these words, for according to the tenor of these words I have made a covenant with you and with Israel.' 28 So he was there with the LORD forty days and forty nights; he neither ate bread nor drank water. And He wrote on the tablets the words of the covenant, the Ten Commandments." Exo. 34:27,28

Through the work God gave to Moses, <u>men's hearts</u> were proven right before the Lord.

5 "Take from among you an offering to the LORD. Whoever *is* of <u>a willing heart</u>, let him bring it as an offering to the LORD: gold, silver, and bronze. . ." 21 "Then everyone came whose <u>heart was stirred</u>, and everyone whose spirit was willing, *and* they brought the LORD's offering for the work of the tabernacle of meeting, for all its service, and for the holy garments. . ." 26 "And all the women <u>whose hearts</u> stirred with wisdom spun yarn of goats' *hair.*" 29 "The children of Israel brought a freewill offering to the LORD, all the men and women <u>whose hearts</u> were willing to bring *material* for all kinds of work which the LORD, by the hand of Moses, had commanded to be done." Exo. 35:5,21,26, and 29

Through Moses God gave the children of Israel, and the world after them, the Law of God and the government God recommended men should follow. Moses is to be set apart as special to the Lord because of his work on earth with men.

JOSHUA

Now before crossing the Jordan, conquests east of Jordan were made, and two tribes and a half were provided for. Then after the death of Moses Joshua the son of Nun, Moses minister, commanded the people how they were to cross the Jordan and when.

"Hear O Israel: Thou art to pass over Jordan this day, to go in to possess nations greater and mightier than thy self, cities great and fenced up to heaven." Deut. 9:1

"For the Lord your God dried up the waters of Jordan from before you, until ye were passed over, as the Lord your God did to the Red Sea, which he dried up from before us ,until we were gone over: That all the people of the earth might know the Hand of the Lord, that it is mighty: that ye might fear the Lord your God forever." Jos. 4: 23,24

After Jericho's fall by the hand of the Lord, Joshua then continued to conquer Ai, Gibeon, and then the five Kings of Southern Canaan.

16 "Thus Joshua took all this land: the mountain country, all the South, all the land of Goshen, the lowland, and the Jordan plain—the mountains of Israel and its lowlands, 17 from Mount Halak and the ascent to Seir, even as far as Baal Gad in the Valley of Lebanon below Mount Hermon. He captured all their kings, and struck them down and killed them. 18 Joshua made war a long time with all those kings. 19 There was not a city that made peace with the children of Israel, except the Hivites, the inhabitants of Gibeon. All *the others* they took in battle. 20 For it was of the LORD to harden their hearts, that they should come against Israel in battle, that He might utterly destroy them, *and* that they might receive no mercy, but that He might destroy them, as the LORD had commanded Moses. 21 And at that time Joshua came and cut off the Anakim from the mountains: from Hebron, from Debir, from Anab, from all the mountains of Judah, and from all the mountains of Israel; Joshua utterly destroyed them with their cities. 22 None of the Anakim were left in the land of the children of Israel; they remained only in Gaza, in Gath, and in Ashdod. 23 So Joshua took the whole land, according to all that the LORD had said to Moses; and Joshua gave it as an inheritance to Israel according to their divisions by their tribes. Then the land rested from war." Jos.11:16-23

All the tribes received their inheritance and the Warriors of the Trans-Jordan Tribes were sent back east of the Jordan.

THE HEART OF JOSHUA

Joshua was one of the heads of the children of Israel who alone with Caleb gave an encouraging word for the capture of Canaan because he saw the land and the people and nevertheless believed God would give the land to Israel. He was apparently chosen by God to lead the entry of Israel across the Jordan because of his belief that God would do what He said. Again Joshua's heart is not mentioned in the word, but it is said over and over that God spoke to him because he listened and obeyed, the following are a few examples:

After the death of Moses the servant of the LORD, it came to pass that the LORD spoke to Joshua the son of Nun, Moses' assistant, saying: 2 "Moses

My servant is dead. Now therefore, arise, go over this Jordan, you and all this people, to the land which I am giving to them—the children of Israel. 3 Every place that the sole of your foot will tread upon I have given you, as I said to Moses." 7 "Only be strong and very courageous, that you may observe to do according to all the law which Moses My servant commanded you; do not turn from it to the right hand or to the left, that you may prosper wherever you go." Josh. 1:1-3,7
And it came to pass, when all the people had completely crossed over the Jordan, that the LORD spoke to Joshua. 4 "Then Joshua called the twelve men whom he had appointed from the children of Israel, one man from every tribe." 8 "And the children of Israel did so, just as Joshua commanded, and took up twelve stones from the midst of the Jordan, as the LORD had spoken to Joshua, according to the number of the tribes of the children of Israel, and carried them over with them to the place where they lodged, and laid them down there." Josh. 4:1,4,8

<u>What can be said about Joshua's heart other than he listened to God</u> and obeyed God. Joshua was trustworthy and true, that is the lesson of Joshua.

23 "So Joshua took the whole land, according to all that the LORD had said to Moses; and Joshua gave it as an inheritance to Israel according to their divisions by their tribes. Then the land rested from war." Josh. 11:23

"After that <u>He gave *them* judges for about four hundred and fifty years, until Samuel</u> the prophet. 21 And afterward they asked for a king; <u>so God gave them Saul</u> the son of Kish, a man of the tribe of Benjamin, for forty years. 22 <u>And when He had removed him, He raised up for them David as king</u>, to whom also He gave testimony and said, '*I have found David the son of Jesse, <u>a man after My own heart, who will do all My will</u>.*' 23 From this man's seed, according to *the* promise, God raised up for Israel a Savior—Jesus." Acts 13:20-23

SAMUEL

Between the death of Joshua and birth of Samuel came "Shopetim" meaning the time of Judges or ruling leaders, accounting for that period, no heart of man was exposed as was Samuel's heart, he was the last of the ruling Judges. Samuel was Mine from heaven 'til he finished his work for Me. His obedience was from his beginning and I never found fault with him. I gave him a heart for Me and he was true to all I asked of him. Seldom have I found a man that was like My Samuel, yes I established him as a prophet of the Lord.

So Samuel grew, and the LORD was with him and let none of his words fall to the ground. 20 "And all Israel from Dan to Beersheba knew that Samuel *had been* established as a prophet of the LORD. 21 Then the LORD appeared again in Shiloh. For the LORD revealed Himself to Samuel in Shiloh by the word of the Lord." 1 Sam. 3:19-21

I came and stood by him and revealed Myself to him many times because Israel was a rebellious lot and they clamored for a King, so they could be like the heathen nations. Samuel was My guiding arm at that time, but events came about against My Servant Samuel as he attempted to quell rebellion. So Samuel was replaced by a king that pleased the nation Israel, but not Samuel or I. At the failures of Saul, I sent Samuel out to pick a King after My own heart David.

35 "Then I will raise up for Myself a faithful priest *who* shall do according to what *is* in My heart and in My mind. I will build him a sure house, and he shall walk before My anointed forever." 1 Sam. 2:35 15 "And Samuel judged Israel all the days of his life. 16 He went from year to year on a circuit to Bethel, Gilgal, and Mizpah, and judged Israel in all those places. 17 But he always returned to Ramah, for his home *was* there. There he judged Israel, and there he built an altar to the Lord." 1 Sam. 7:15-17

KINGS OF JUDAH

The following examples of men's hearts are shown by examination of the Kings of Judah. <u>Remembering the purpose of this book is to teach the children of today about the necessity of watching over their heart</u> as they seek a closer walk with Jesus and our Heavenly Father. I am giving men all over the earth the same lessons today that the children of old received, do not believe that your trials and tribulations are substantially any different than to what I subjected the children of Israel. From Adam on, men have not changed, they all have a spirit, soul, and a body, and they all are in Our Image and Likeness. If you would be wise then learn from the lessons given to My dear ones of the past, and pattern your walk to avoid self-pleasing issues of your walk with Me. This Book is filled with God pleasing ways and I do not hide "The Way" for My children of the present. I do have blessings, especially for the obedient ones of today at this time, because the time is so short and I desire to give "Spurt Growth" as rewards to those who will rise up to the challenges I set before them. Remember to whom much is given much is required, so temper your walk with great care. These books, along with others in this series, are especially for the lifting up and edifying the Bride of Christ.

SAUL

I chose Saul because he would please the people of Israel, and I gave them to understand, through Samuel, if they did not forsake Me I would watch over and keep them safe. I promised Saul the Spirit of the Lord would come upon him and he would show himself to be a prophet. Now Saul was a self-driven man who in a crises time gave way to following self's urgings rather than following the Lord's directions. Saul sinned by offering burnt offering, which he was forbidden to do, thus he lost his Kingdom. It can be said Saul's heart was never completely right before the Lord.

23 "So they ran and brought him from there; and when he stood among the people, he was taller than any of the people from his shoulders upward. 24 And Samuel said to all the people, 'Do you see him whom the LORD has chosen, that *there is* no one like him among all the people?' So all the people shouted and said, 'Long live the king!' 25 Then Samuel explained to the people the behavior of royalty, and wrote *it* in a book and laid *it* up before the LORD. And Samuel sent all the people away, every man to his house. 26 And Saul also went home to Gibeah; and valiant *men* went with him, whose hearts God had touched." 1 Sam. 10:23-26

6 "Then the Spirit of the LORD will come upon you, and you will proph-

esy with them and be turned into another man. [7] And let it be, when these signs come to you, *that* you do as the occasion demands; for God *is* with you. [8] You shall go down before me to Gilgal; and surely I will come down to you to offer burnt offerings *and* make sacrifices of peace offerings. Seven days you shall wait, till I come to you and show you what you should do. [9] So it was, when he had turned his back to go from Samuel, that God gave him another heart; and all those signs came to pass that day." 1 Sam. 10;6-9

[14] "Then Samuel said to the people, 'Come, let us go to Gilgal and renew the kingdom there.' [15] So all the people went to Gilgal, and there they made Saul king before the LORD in Gilgal. There they made sacrifices of peace offerings before the LORD, and there Saul and all the men of Israel rejoiced greatly." 1 Sam. 11:14,15

[8] "Then he waited seven days, according to the time set by Samuel. But Samuel did not come to Gilgal; and the people were scattered from him. [9] So Saul said, 'Bring a burnt offering and peace offerings here to me.' And he offered the burnt offering. [10] Now it happened, as soon as he had finished presenting the burnt offering, that Samuel came; and Saul went out to meet him, that he might greet him. [11] And Samuel said, 'What have you done?' Saul said, 'When I saw that the people were scattered from me, and *that* you did not come within the days appointed, and *that* the Philistines gathered together at Michmash, [12] then I said, 'The Philistines will now come down on me at Gilgal, and I have not made supplication to the LORD.' Therefore I felt compelled, and offered a burnt offering.' [13] And Samuel said to Saul, 'You have done foolishly. You have not kept the commandment of the LORD your God, which He commanded you. For now the LORD would have established your kingdom over Israel forever. [14] But now your kingdom shall not continue. The LORD has sought for Himself a man after His own heart, and the LORD has commanded him *to be* commander over His people, because you have not kept what the LORD commanded you." 1 Sam. 13:8-14

DAVID

I called David from before his birthing to be a man after My own heart. All of My plans executed come from eternity past to be flushed out in physical reality. Man never knows or sees all that I do, only My children of forever will know in fullness of time. David I called to be My Prince of the Kingdom of Eternity. His heart was given him to obey and work out to My satisfaction. Few children are so selected in this manner, so guidance to My children for their control of purpose does not come in such a manner. The study of David should be taken with the purpose of exposing man's frailties and man's victories. All victories should expose My guidance of events.

David's battles in the flesh should give guidance to all who will properly analyze and make inquiry into the how's and why's of such events. Many are the pressures that push and pull My children. I am using every happening to its full advantage to each child of Mine. Never think, believe, or feel that I'm not present or in control. The events molding and forming David as My prince are his alone, but a study of David's walk with Me should be most fulfilling and helpful to anyone who takes the time and advantage to learn from it. So dear children, seeking My heart and ways will find comforting guidance from David's life. Pay attention to the words of his Psalm's, they will bless you as they still do Me.

1 "Then all the tribes of Israel came to David at Hebron and spoke, saying, 'Indeed we *are* your bone and your flesh. 2 Also, in time past, when Saul was king over us, you were the one who led Israel out and brought them in; and the LORD said to you, <u>'You shall shepherd My people Israel, and be ruler over Israel.</u>' " 3 Therefore all the elders of Israel came to the king at Hebron, and King David made a covenant with them at Hebron before the LORD. <u>And they anointed David king over Israel</u>. 4 David *was* thirty years old when he began to reign, *and* he reigned forty years. 5 In Hebron he reigned over Judah seven years and six months, and in Jerusalem he reigned thirty-three years over all Israel and Judah." 2 Sam. 5:1-5

8 "Now therefore, thus shall you say to My servant David, 'Thus says the LORD of hosts: 'I took you from the sheepfold, from following the sheep, to be ruler over My people, over Israel. 9 And I have been with you wherever you have gone, and have cut off all your enemies from before you, and have made you a great name, like the name of the great men who *are* on the earth. 10 Moreover I will appoint a place for My people Israel, and will plant them, that they may dwell in a place of their own and move no more; nor shall the sons of wickedness oppress them anymore, as previously, 11 since the time that I commanded judges *to be* over My people Israel, and have caused you to rest from all your enemies.' Also the LORD tells you that He will make you a house.

12 When your days are fulfilled and you rest with your fathers, I will set up your seed after you, who will come from your body, and I will establish his kingdom. 13 He shall build a house for My name, and I will establish the throne of his kingdom forever." 2 Sam.7:8-13

Then David spoke to the LORD the words of this song, on the day when the LORD had delivered him from the hand of all his enemies, and from the hand of Saul. 2 And he said: "The LORD *is* my rock and my fortress and my deliverer; 3 The God of my strength, in whom I will trust; My shield and the horn of my salvation,

My stronghold and my refuge; My Savior, You save me from violence. 4 I will call upon the LORD, *who is worthy* to be praised; So shall I be saved from my enemies." 2 Sam. 22:1-4

22 "For I have kept the ways of the LORD, And have not wickedly departed from my God. 23 For all His judgments *were* before me; And *as for* His statutes, I did not depart from them. 24 I was also blameless before Him, And I kept myself from my iniquity. 25 Therefore the LORD has recompensed me according to my righteousness, According to my cleanness in His eyes." 2 Sam.22:22-25

Now these *are* the last words of David. *Thus* says David the son of Jesse; "*Thus* says the man raised up on high, The anointed of the God of Jacob,

And the sweet psalmist of Israel: 2 "The Spirit of the LORD spoke by me, And His word *was* on my tongue. 3The God of Israel said, The Rock of Israel spoke to me: 'He who rules over men *must be* just." 2 Sam. 23:1-3

3 Now the days of David drew near that he should die, and he charged Solomon his son, saying: 2 "I go the way of all the earth; be strong, therefore, and prove yourself a man. 3 And keep the charge of the LORD your God: to walk in His ways, to keep His statutes, His commandments, His judgments, and His testimonies, as it is written in the Law of Moses, that you may prosper in all that you do and wherever you turn." 1 Kings 2:1-3

SOLOMON

24 "Then David comforted Bathsheba his wife, and went in to her and lay with her. So she bore a son, and he called his name Solomon. Now the LORD loved him, 25 and He sent *word* by the hand of Nathan the prophet: So he called his name Jedidiah, because of the LORD." 2 Sam. 12:24,25

11 "The period that David reigned over Israel *was* forty years; seven years he reigned in Hebron, and in Jerusalem he reigned thirty-three years. 12 Then Solomon sat on the throne of his father David; and his kingdom was firmly established." 1 Kings 2:11,12

Yes, I loved the son of David as one of My own. I kept him close to bless, lead, and guide him in all of his ways. My children can learn much to help their walk with Me by paying attention to the many ways of Solomon. Yes I loved him as I had loved Adam and many who followed after him. My love and calling goes out from My heart of love to bless, teach, guide, and keep, but free will I've given and free will has its opposition to Me. I will not bow My heart's desire to the way of free will for I call no man who has a seed of doubt or opposition in him about Me. The free will is My gift to all My children of Eternity for it is their safety forever that is being protected. No entrance will ever be given to evil, even as a seed in the heart of one of My children, that would contaminate Our Eternity of love in peace. All I do is for this purpose of having My Family pure and uncontaminated forever. As I have lost Adam, I have lost many children by their own choice, so dear ones if there is any lesson to be learned from

Solomon's heart take his example and learn your lesson well!

17 "Now it was in the heart of my father David to build a temple for the name of the LORD God of Israel. 18 But the LORD said to my father David, 'Whereas it was in your heart to build a temple for My name, you did well that it was in your heart. 19 Nevertheless you shall not build the temple, but your son who will come from your body, he shall build the temple for My name.' 20 So the LORD has fulfilled His word which He spoke; and I have filled the position of my father David, and sit on the throne of Israel, as the LORD promised; and I have built a temple for the name of the LORD God of Israel. 21 And there I have made a place for the ark, in which *is* the covenant of the LORD which He made with our fathers, when He brought them out of the land of Egypt." 1 Kings 8:17-21

But King Solomon loved many foreign women, as well as the daughter of Pharaoh: women of the Moabites, Ammonites, Edomites, Sidonians, *and* Hittites— 2 "··· from the nations of whom the LORD had said to the children of Israel, '. . .You shall not intermarry with them, nor they with you. Surely they will turn away your hearts after their gods.' Solomon clung to these in love. 3 And he had seven hundred wives, princesses, and three hundred concubines; and his wives turned away his heart. 4 For it was so, when Solomon was old, that his wives turned his heart after other gods; and his heart was not loyal to the LORD his God, as *was* the heart of his father David. 5 For Solomon went after Ashtoreth the goddess of the Sidonians, and after Milcom the abomination of the Ammonites. 6 Solomon did evil in the sight of the LORD, and did not fully follow the LORD, as *did* his father David." 1 Kings 11:1-6

39 "And I will afflict the descendants of David because of this, but not forever.' 40 Solomon therefore sought to kill Jeroboam. But Jeroboam arose and fled to Egypt, to Shishak King of Egypt, and was in Egypt until the death of Solomon. 41 Now the rest of the acts of Solomon, all that he did, and his wisdom, *are* they not written in the book of the acts of Solomon? 42 And the period that Solomon reigned in Jerusalem over all Israel *was* forty years." 1 Kings 11:39-42

REHOBOAM

Rehoboam was Solomon's son, a son of David, so I extended David's blessings onto him, <u>but his heart was filled with self</u> and it left little for Me to work with. For Israel's sake I kept the kingdom as free from his sinful ways as he allowed, but punish him I must. <u>My dear children of today learn your lessons from the son's of David </u>as We walk through these scriptures together. This son of Solomon started out on a downward path of his own choosing by not listening to the Elders of his father' reign, but<u> he sought to please himself </u>and the young men he had grown up with. His actions caused Israel to be in rebellion against the house of David. Rehoboam appointed for himself priests for high places for demons and calf idols that he made. He made some good moves strengthening the kingdom for three years then he forsook the law of the Lord. He did evil <u>because he did not prepare his heart to seek the Lord</u>.

Now it came to pass, when Rehoboam had established the kingdom and had strengthened himself, that <u>he forsook the law of the LORD</u>, and all Israel along with him. 2 Chron. 12;1

Thus King Rehoboam strengthened himself in Jerusalem and reigned. Now Rehoboam *was* forty-one years old when he became king; and he reigned seventeen years in Jerusalem, the city which the LORD had chosen out of all the tribes of Israel, to put His name there. His mother's name *was* Naamah, an Ammonitess. [14] <u>"And he did evil, because he did not prepare his heart to seek the LORD.</u> [15] The acts of Rehoboam, first and last, *are* they not written in the book of Shemaiah the prophet, and of Iddo the seer concerning genealogies? And *there were* wars between Rehoboam and Jeroboam all their days. [16] So Rehoboam rested with his fathers, and was buried in the City of David. Then Abijah his son reigned in his place." 2 Chron. 12:13-16

ABIJAH, ASA, AND JEHOSHAPHAT

These three sons of David did a better job of reigning because they had not forsaken the Lord and they did good and right <u>with all their heart</u>, still they failed in many ways, but the Lord favored them because of David.

4 "Then <u>Abijah</u> stood on Mount Zemaraim, which *is* in the mountains of Ephraim, and said, "Hear me, Jeroboam and all Israel: 5 Should you not know that <u>the LORD God of Israel gave the dominion over Israel to David forever,</u> to him and his sons, by a covenant of salt?" 10 "But as for us, <u>the LORD *is* our God, and we have not forsaken Him;</u> and the priests who minister to the LORD *are* the sons of Aaron, and the Levites *attend* to *their* duties. 11 And they burn to the LORD every morning and every evening burnt sacrifices and sweet incense; *they* also *set* the showbread *in order on* the pure *gold* table, and the lamp stand of gold with its lamps to burn every evening; for <u>we keep the command of the LORD our God,</u> but you have forsaken Him." 2 Chron. 13:4,5,10, 11

<u>So Abijah rested with his fathers,</u> and they buried him in the City of David. Then <u>Asa his son reigned in his place.</u> In his days the land was quiet for ten years. 2 "<u>Asa did *what was* good and right in the eyes of the LORD his God,</u> 3 for he removed the altars of the foreign *gods* and the high places, and broke down the *sacred* pillars and cut down the wooden images. 4 He commanded Judah to seek the LORD God of their fathers, and to observe the law and the commandment. 5 He also removed the high places and the incense altars from all the cities of Judah, and the kingdom was quiet under him." 2 Chron. 14:1-5

10 "So they gathered together at Jerusalem in the third month, in the fifteenth year of <u>the reign of Asa.</u> 11 And they offered to the LORD at that time seven hundred bulls and seven thousand sheep from the spoil they had brought. 12 <u>Then they entered into a covenant to seek the LORD God of their fathers with all their heart and with all their soul;</u> 13 and whoever would not seek the LORD God of Israel was to be put to death, whether small or great, whether man or woman." 17 "But the high places were not removed from Israel. Nevertheless <u>the heart of Asa was loyal all his day.</u>" 2 Chron. 15: 10-13,17

12 "And in the thirty-ninth year of his reign, Asa became diseased in his feet, and his malady was severe; yet in his disease <u>he did not seek the LORD,</u> but the physicians. 13 So <u>Asa rested with his fathers; he died in the</u>

<u>forty-first year of his reign</u>. [14] They buried him in his own tomb, which he had made for himself in the City of David; and they laid him in the bed which was filled with spices and various ingredients prepared in a mixture of ointments. They made a very great burning for him." 2 Chron. 16:12-14

Then Jehoshaphat his son reigned in his place, and strengthened himself against Israel. [2] "And he placed troops in all the fortified cities of Judah, and set garrisons in the land of Judah and in the cities of Ephraim which Asa his father had taken. [3] Now <u>the LORD was with Jehoshaphat, because he walked in the former ways of his father David;</u> he did not seek the Baals, [4] but sought the God of his father, and walked in His commandments and not according to the acts of Israel. [5] Therefore the LORD established the kingdom in his hand; and all Judah gave presents to Jehoshaphat, and he had riches and honor in abundance. [6] <u>And his heart took delight in the ways of the LORD</u>; moreover he removed the high places and wooden images from Judah." 2 Chron. 17: 1-6

JOASH, AMAZIAH, UZZIAH, AND JOTHAM

These four sons of David, Kings of Judah, are all ones who tried to be what they should be, and I watched over them carefully. Each one tried to do right, but <u>self and self-pleasing was too strong for most of them</u>, however Jotham was kept close to the Lord and he finished well for his short time.

JOASH

<u>Joash</u> *was* seven years old when he became king, and he reigned forty years in Jerusalem. His mother's name *was* Zibiah of Beersheba. [2] "Joash <u>did *what was* right in the sight of the LORD all the days of Jehoiada the priest.</u> [3] And Jehoiada took two wives for him, and he had sons and daughters. [4] Now it happened after this *that* <u>Joash set his heart</u> on repairing the house of the LORD." 2 Chron. 24:1-4

24 "For the army of the Syrians came with a small company of men; but the LORD delivered a very great army into their hand, <u>because they had forsaken the LORD God of their fathers. So they executed judgment against Joash</u>. 25 And when they had withdrawn from him (for they left him severely wounded), his own servants conspired against him because of the blood of the sons of Jehoiada the priest, and <u>killed him on his bed. So he died</u>. And they buried him in the City of David, but they did not bury him in the tombs of the kings. 26 These are the ones who conspired against him: Zabad the son of Shimeath the Ammonitess, and Jehozabad the son of Shimrith the Moabitess. 27 Now *concerning* his sons, and the many oracles about him, and the repairing of the house of God, indeed they *are* written in the annals of the book of the kings. Then <u>Amaziah his son reigned in his place</u>." 2 Chron. 24:24-27

AMAZIAH

Amaziah *was* twenty-five years old *when* he became king, and he reigned twenty-nine years in Jerusalem. His mother's name *was* Jehoaddan of Jerusalem. 2 "And <u>he did *what was* right in the sight of the LORD, but not with a loyal heart.</u>" 2 Chron. 25: 1,2

7 "But a man of God came to him, saying, 'O king, do not let the army of Israel go with you, for the LORD *is* not with Israel—*not with* any of the children of Ephraim. 8 But if you go, be gone! Be strong in battle! *Even so,* <u>God shall make you fall before the enemy</u>; for God has power to help and to overthrow.'" 14 "Now it was so, after Amaziah came from the slaughter of the Edomites, that <u>he brought the gods of the people of Seir, set them up *to be* his gods</u>, and bowed down before them and burned incense to them. 15 <u>Therefore the anger of the LORD was aroused against Amaziah,</u> and He sent him a prophet who said to him, 'Why have you sought the gods of the people, which could not rescue their own people from your hand?'" 2 Chron. 25:7,8,14,15

25 <u>Amaziah the son of Joash,</u> king of Judah, lived fifteen years after the death of Joash the son of Jehoahaz, king of Israel. 26 "Now the rest of the

acts of Amaziah, from first to last, indeed *are* they not written in the book of the kings of Judah and Israel? 27 <u>After the time that Amaziah turned away from following the LORD,</u> they made a conspiracy against him in Jerusalem, and he fled to Lachish; but they sent after him to Lachish and killed him there. 28 Then they brought him on horses and buried him with his fathers in the City of Judah." 2 Chron. 25:25-28

UZZIAH

Now all the people of Judah took <u>Uzziah,</u> who *was* sixteen years old, and made him king instead of his father Amaziah. 2 "He built Elath and restored it to Judah, after the king rested with his fathers. 3 <u>Uzziah</u> *was* sixteen years old when he became king, and he reigned fifty-two years in Jerusalem. His mother's name was Jecholiah of Jerusalem. 4 And <u>he did *what was* right in the sight of the LORD</u>, according to all that his father Amaziah had done. 5 He sought God in the days of Zechariah, who had understanding in the visions of God; and <u>as long as he sought the LORD, God made him prosper."</u> 2 Chron. 26:1-5

16 "<u>But when he was strong his heart was lifted up</u>, to *his* destruction, for <u>he transgressed against the LORD </u>his God by entering the temple of the LORD to burn incense on the altar of incense. 17 So Azariah the priest went in after him, and with him were eighty priests of the LORD—valiant men. 18 And they withstood <u>King Uzziah</u>, and said to him, "*It is* not for you, Uzziah, to burn incense to the LORD, but for the priests, the sons of Aaron, who are consecrated to burn incense. Get out of the sanctuary, for you have trespassed! <u>You *shall have* no honor from the LORD God</u>."

19 Then Uzziah became furious; and he *had* a censer in his hand to burn incense. And while he was angry with the priests, <u>leprosy broke out on his forehead</u>, before the priests in the house of the LORD, beside the incense altar20 And Azariah the chief priest and all the priests looked at him, and there, on his forehead, he *was* leprous; so they thrust him out of that place. Indeed he also hurried to get out, because the LORD had struck him

21 <u>King Uzziah was a leper</u> until the day of his death. He dwelt in an isolated house, because he was a leper; for he was cut off from the house of

the LORD. Then Jotham his son *was* over the king's house, judging the people of the land. 22 Now the rest of the acts of Uzziah, from first to last, the prophet Isaiah the son of Amoz wrote. 23 So Uzziah rested with his fathers, and they buried him with his fathers in the field of burial which *belonged* to the kings, for they said, "He is a leper." <u>Then Jotham his son reigned</u> in his place." 2 Chron. 26:16-23

JOTHAM

<u>Jotham *was* twenty-five years old when he became king</u>, and he reigned sixteen years in Jerusalem. His mother's name *was* Jerushah the daughter of Zadok. 2 "And <u>he did *what was* right in the sight of the LORD</u>, according to all that his father Uzziah had done (although he did not enter the temple of the LORD). But still the people acted corruptly." 6 "So <u>Jotham became mighty, because he prepared his ways before the LORD his God.</u> 7 Now the rest of the acts of Jotham, and all his wars and his ways, indeed they *are* written in the book of the kings of Israel and Judah. 8 He was twenty-five years old when he became king, and he reigned sixteen years in Jerusalem. 9 So Jotham rested with his fathers, and they buried him in the City of David. Then <u>Ahaz his son reigned in his place.</u>" 2 Chron. 27:1,2,6-9

THE CAUSE OF THE BABYLONIAN CAPTIVITY

As the people of Israel followed the examples of their rulers, it is shown vividly by the downfall of their kingdom. All of My children in every age must <u>pay more attention to each ones "Heart" condition</u>. The study of the lives of the many kings such as David, Asa, Jehoshaphat, Joash, Jotham and Josiah shows they were outstanding kings for their time and place, because they, each one, attempted to <u>watch over their heart</u> for Me, they did well despite their defects.

These rulers saved the nation from destruction for a long period of time. However the large majority of monarchs did not live on the high plane of righteousness, but slipped into gross sin and idolatry, which brought upon divine judgments, and ended in the captivity of Babylon. The books of Ezra, Nehemah, Esther, and Job find few references to God's heart and man's heart, but in the Psalms and Proverbs both are given many references, some are worthy of mention:

GOD'S AND MAN'S HEART IN THE PSALMS AND PROVERBS
[Not every reference is listed]

Using the Psalms and Proverbs for your heart lessons <u>requires you to first talk to Me.</u> I will then be able to lead and guide you with understanding. All of your learning now should be a "quick study type" because of the short time left. So dear ones <u>come to Me in Our quiet time</u>, and then We can fulfill Our pact together. Every lesson may not be yours because they touch all hearts, some needing more or less of the lessons. <u>By drawing Me into your learning desires</u> means I can point out where your greatest needs lie and skip these areas you have no need of. Confirm with Me your growth desires, share with Me where you want to be, and how much you want to be used. With this kind of honesty there is no end to Our Wonderful Walk together.

Read slowly each line and <u>invite Me to bring understanding into your heart</u> when a sentence or word particularly touches you. All of your growth is to <u>come into your heart</u> [your born-again new creation] <u>first</u>. Do not look for or expect your mind to be where I will bring complete understanding, no I will instruct <u>your heart first</u>; this is the way to have the mind of Jesus. Pray for this and believe We, together, can bring it to pass.

My dear children I want you to understand all of My children <u>are Spirits</u> working in a physical environment, <u>not physical beings</u> trying to enter into the Spirit Realm. Let his word penetrate from your heart [spirit] into your mind. This is your true situation, you were given a soul with a "self" to lead and guide you back into your Spirit realm. Your soul must shed "self" after being saved, after a "born again" experience. Remember, 1 Thess. 5:23,24.

You are spirit and soul and body, all to be found blameless at the coming of Lord Jesus Christ." Faithful is He Who is calling you to Himself and

He is utterly trustworthy. There is something you should know about your mind. The mind is the battleground of your warfare, <u>with sin, with self and with Satan</u>. Self is a supporter of flesh, self-pleasing is self's desire that's why after your new birth self must diminish then disappear; to be replaced with Jesus.

3 "For though we walk in the flesh, we do not war according to the flesh. 4 For the weapons of our warfare *are* not carnal but mighty in God for pulling down strongholds, 5 casting down arguments and every high thing that exalts itself against the knowledge of God, <u>bringing every thought into captivity to the obedience of Christ,</u> 6 and being ready to punish all disobedience when your obedience is fulfilled." 2 Cor. 10:3-6

<u>*There is* therefore now no condemnation to those who are in Christ Jesus, who do not walk according to the flesh, but according to the Spirit</u>. 2 "For the law of the Spirit of life in Christ Jesus has made me free from the law of sin and death . . ." 4 ". . .that the righteous requirement of the law might be fulfilled in us who do not walk according to the flesh but according to the Spirit. 5 <u>For those who live according to the flesh set their minds on the things of the flesh</u>, but those *who live* according to the Spirit, the things of the Spirit." Rom. 8:1,2,4,5

13 "For if you live according to the flesh you will die; but <u>if by the Spirit you put to death the deeds of the body, you will live</u>. 14 <u>For as many as are led by the Spirit of God, these are sons of God,</u> 15 For you did not receive the spirit of bondage again to fear, but you received the Spirit of adoption by whom we cry out, Abba, Father." Rom. 8:13-15

I beseech you therefore, brethren, by the mercies of God, that you present your bodies a living sacrifice, holy, acceptable to God, *which is* your reasonable service. 2 "And do not be conformed to this world, but be transformed by the renewing of your mind, that you may prove what *is* that good and acceptable and perfect will of God." Rom. 12:1,2

You must come to understand self must die, kill self, and replace it with the Lord Jesus Christ! This is the only assurance that your heart is right with your precious Heavenly Father!

THE PSALMS—MEN'S HEART

This short walk through the Psalms should not mean a hasty one for you, remember this book is to be your tool lifting you into a closer walk and a high position in the eyes of the Lord. Do not think fast and quick is My way dear children. I never am rushed, I never have been pushed by haste, and all I do is in decency and "In Order." To be timely is to be prepared and planned in advance, so quick catch-ups are never necessary. Learn to meditate on My truth, call on Me and We will have a wonderful time together as you grow in knowledge and wisdom. They will be your companions forever as you learn to listen, believe, and obey.

The upright in heart <u>are saved</u>. Ps. 7:10; The upright seek God with their <u>whole heart</u>. Ps. 9:1; They <u>say to their heart or speak to their heart</u>. Ps. 10:6,11; Fools have <u>double hearts</u>. Ps. 12:2; Fools have said to their hearts "<u>There is no God</u>." Ps. 14:1; God <u>proves man's heart, and tries man's heart</u>. Ps. 17:3; Those who seek God will praise the Lord, <u>let his heart live forever</u>. Ps. 22:26; When the Lord is man's light and salvation his <u>heart shall not fear</u>. Ps. 27:3; The righteous shall be glad and rejoice all who are <u>upright in heart</u>. Ps.32:11; The mouth of the righteous speaks wisdom, his tongue talks of justice, and he <u>has the law of God in his heart</u>. Ps. 37:30,31; God knows the <u>secrets of man's heart</u>. Ps. 44:21; God can create a <u>clean heart in man as he asks for it</u>. Ps. 73:1; God has turned away His anger when man's heart was not steadfast with Him, for He remembered <u>they were but flesh</u>. Ps. 78:37,39; If men's hearts goes astray, and they do not know God's ways, <u>they shall not enter His rest</u>. Ps.95:10,11; Light is sown for the upright, and <u>gladness for the upright</u> in heart. Ps. 97:11; I will walk within my house with <u>a perfect heart</u>. Ps. 101:2; <u>A perverse heart</u> shall depart from me, I will not know wickedness. Ps. 101:4; The one who has a haughty look and <u>a proud heart him I will not endure</u>. Ps. 101:5; Glory in His name, <u>let the hearts of those rejoice</u> who seek the Lord. Ps. 105:3; I will <u>praise the Lord with my whole heart</u>. Ps. 111:1; Your word <u>have I hidden in my heart</u>, that I might not sin against You. Ps. 119:11; I <u>have inclined my heart</u> to perform your statutes forever, to the very end. Ps. 119:112; Search me, Oh God, and <u>know my heart.</u> Ps. 139:23; <u>Do not incline</u> my heart to evil to do any evil thing. Ps. 141:4; He <u>heals the broken-hearted</u> and binds up their wounds. Ps. 147:3.

The proper use of the words here shown would be to take each pronouncement given and meditate on it, asking Me to teach and train you in the correct use of God's word. Only deliberate concentration on the one subject at a time will show the growth that comes from this type of study.

THE PROVERBS—MEN'S HEART

The proverbs are given to My children <u>straight from My heart to your heart</u>, so grasp the help here shown to you, and you will surely be blessed by your careful study with a <u>believing heart</u>. Here is a brief look through My Bible's Book pf Proverbs; <u>remembering We are studying Our Hearts</u>, so learn how to prepare your heart for Our Eternity by your slow and careful attention to blessing your heart through obedience to the Word.

Proverbs 2:1,2
"My son, if you receive My words, and treasure My commands within you, so incline your ear to wisdom, and <u>apply your heart to understanding</u>."

Proverbs 2:10
"<u>When wisdom enters your heart</u>, and knowledge is pleasant to your soul, discretion will preserve you, and understanding will keep you."

Proverbs 3:1
"My son, do not forget My law, but <u>let your heart</u> keep My commands."

Proverbs 3:3
"Let not mercy and truth forsake you, bind them around your neck, <u>write them on the tablet of your heart</u>."

Proverbs 3:5
"Trust in the Lord <u>with all your heart</u>, and lean not on your own understanding."

Proverbs 4:4
"He also taught me, and said to me, <u>Let your heart retain My words.</u>"

Proverbs 4:20,21
"My son, give attention to My words, incline your ear to My sayings, do not let them depart from your eyes, <u>keep them in the midst of your heart.</u>"

Proverbs 4:23
"<u>Keep you heart with all diligence</u>, for out of it spring the issues of life."

Proverbs 6:14

"<u>Perversity is in his heart</u>, he devises evil continually, he sows discord."

Proverbs 6:18

"The Lord hates <u>a heart that devises wicked plans</u>, feet that are swift in running to evil."

Proverbs 6:24,25

"To keep you from evil women, from the flattering tongue of a seductress, <u>do not lust after her beauty in your heart.</u>"

Proverbs 7:2,3

"Keep God's words and His commands, bind them on your fingers, <u>write them on th tablet of your heart.</u>"

Proverbs 8:5

"Wisdom cries out. Oh you simple ones, understand prudence, and you fools, <u>be of an understanding heart</u>."

Proverbs 10:8

"<u>The wise in heart will receive commands</u>, but a prating fool will fall."

Proverbs 10:20

"The tongue of the righteous is choice silver, <u>the heart of the wicked is worth little</u>."

Proverbs 11:20

"<u>Those who are of a perverse heart are an abomination to the Lord</u>, but such as are blameless in their ways are His delight."

Proverbs 12:8

"A man will be commended according to his wisdom, but <u>he who is of a perverse heart will be despised.</u>"

Proverbs 12:20

"Deceit is in the heart of those who devise evil, but <u>counselors of peace have joy.</u>"

Proverbs 12:23

"A prudent man conceals knowledge, but <u>the heart of fools proclaims foolishness.</u>"

Proverbs 12:25

"<u>Anxiety in the heart of man causes depression</u>, but a good word makes it glad."

Proverbs 13:12

"<u>Hope deferred makes the heart sick</u>, but when desire comes, it is a tree of life."

Proverbs 14:10

"<u>The heart knows its own bitterness</u>, and a stranger does not share its joy."

Proverbs 14:13

"Even in laughter the heart may sorrow, and the end of mirth may be grief."

Proverbs 14:14

"The backslider in heart will be filled with his own ways, but a good man will be satisfied from above."

Proverbs 14:33

"Wisdom rests quietly in the heart of him who has understanding, but what is in the heart of fools is made known."

Proverbs 15:7

"The lips of the wise disperse knowledge, but the heart of the fool does not do so."

Proverbs 15:13

"A merry heart makes a cheerful countenance, but by sorrow of heart the spirit is broken."

Proverbs 15:14

"The heart of him who has understanding seeks knowledge, but the mouth of fools feeds on foolishness."

Proverbs 15:15

"All of the days of the afflicted are evil, but he who is of a merry heart has a continual feast."

Proverbs 15:28

"The heart of the righteous studies how to answer, but the mouth of the wicked pours forth evil."

Proverbs 15:30

"The light of the eyes rejoices the heart, and a good report makes the bones healthy."

Proverbs 16:1

"The preparations of the heart belong to man, but the answer of the tongue is from the Lord."

Proverbs 16:5

"Everyone who is proud in heart is an abomination to the Lord, though they join forces , none will go unpunished."

Proverbs 16:9

"A man's heart plans his way, but the Lord directs his steps."

Proverbs 16:21

"The wise in heart will be called prudent, and sweetness of the lips increases learning."

Proverbs 16 23
"The heart of the wise teaches his mouth, and adds learning to his lips."
Proverbs 17:16
"Why is there in the hand of a fool the purchase price of wisdom, since he has no heart for it?"
Proverbs 17:20
"He who has a deceitful heart finds no good, and he who has a perverse tongue falls into evil?"
Proverbs 18:2
"A fool has no delight in understanding, but in expressing his own heart."
Proverbs 19:3
"The foolishness of a man twists his way, and his heart frets against the Lord."
Proverbs 19:21
"There are many plans in a man's heart, nevertheless the Lord's counsel— that will stand."
Proverbs 20:5
"Counsel in the heart of man is like deep water, but a man of understanding will draw it out."

Proverbs 20:9
"Who can say, "I have made my heart clean, I am pure from my sin?"
Proverbs 22:11
"He who loves purity of heart and has grace on his lips, the king will be his friend."
Proverbs 22:17
"Incline your ear and hear the words of the wise, and apply your heart to my knowledge."
Proverbs 23:7
"For as he thinks in his heart, so is he."
Proverbs 23:12
"Apply your heart to instructions, and your ears to words of knowledge."
Proverbs 23:15
"My son, if your heart is wise, My heart will rejoice—indeed, I myself." [God]
Proverbs 23:17
"Do not let your heart envy sinners, but in the fear of the Lord continue all day long."

Proverbs 23:19

"Hear, my son, and be wise; and guide your heart in the way."

Proverbs 23:26

"My son, give me your heart, and let our eyes observe my ways."

Proverbs 23:31-33

"Do not look on the wine when it is red, when it sparkles in the cup, when it swirls around smoothly; at the last it bites like a serpent, and stings like a viper, and your eyes will see strange things, and your heart will utter perverse things."

Proverbs 24:1,2

"Do not be envious of evil men, nor desire to be with them; for their heart devises violence, and their lips talk of troublemaking."

Proverbs24:17

"Do not rejoice when your enemy falls, and do not let your heart be glad when he stumbles."

Proverbs 25:20

"Like one who takes away a garment in cold weather, and like vinegar on soda, is one who sings songs to a heavy heart."

Proverbs 27:9

"Ointment and perfume delight the heart, and the sweetness of a man's friend does so by hearty counsel."

Proverbs 27:19

"As in water face reveals face, so man's heart reveals the man."

Proverbs 28:14

"Happy is the man who is always reverent, but he who hardens his heart will fall into calamity."

Proverbs 28:25

"He who is of a proud heart stirs up strife, but he who trusts in the Lord will be prospered."

Proverbs 28:26

"He who trusts in his own heart is a fool, but whoever walks wisely will be delivered."

"All learning is useless for My children unless I am in the middle of it. Call on Me and I will answer, listen to Me, and I will show the deep and wonderful meaning behind the teaching I bring to My loved ones. Only you, dear ones, can make these words of Mine come alive in your hearts!"

ECCLESIASTES

This book brings out a study of man's heart and desires, without ever touching the heart of the Father or His ways or plans. This is not a study to help find God's way, but a look at the worst and best man can do. Man's wisdom, power, education, knowledge, pleasure, influence, and happiness, are all considered, but without God's wisdom and desires, none of the above is worthy of a man's desires <u>who has a heart only for things of Our Father.</u>

SONG OF SOLOMON

In a search for the Heart of God, the Song of Solomon continues in stressing the major themes of warm human emotions and love, but does not carry on to show God's will or way. Man's heart and desires are only expressed to show the human side of marriage and sexual relationships.

ISAIAH

Isaiah speaks of the heart of the kingdom of Judah, saying, "The whole head is sick, and the whole heart is faint [Feeble, Sick, and Nauseated]. Isa. 1;5 A lesson is in that statement for all men who <u>fail to seek God's heart and then change their own heart </u>to follow after God. Isaiah is a man that followed My heart and I have had few men who were more loyal or dedicated in following My plan for them. Many were the hardships and trials for him, but he wavered not, but stayed by all I set before him. The lesson of Isaiah is a study of how I desire My children to seek and keep on seeking, try and keep on trying.

The study of My Bible will show the men who I hold as great in My kingdom, and who are wonderful examples for all to follow. However I alter lives to fit their particular calling in the time and place of their growth. The major lessons can work out to keep each and every child I call, but the best path for each one to follow is, "To be led by My Holy Spirit that I give them, and then be obedient to the school I call them to attend."

Notice the obedience of Isaiah as My prophet, speaking out the words I give him to lead, direct, encourage or denounce as I willed. Children of God, no matter the time or place, should be able to exercise the gifts I freely give them, to serve My purposes not theirs. Learn the things I taught My other children and with obedience leading you, you will avoid many pitfalls and circumstances of harmful nature. Obedience is a path of victory that is only confused and misused by "Self's" intervention. My children's universal lesson is to follow My Spirit's leading, and find protection as your close companion.

JEREMIAH

Jeremiah was My "Weeping Prophet" who I called during the dark days of the Kingdom of Judah. He lived from the thirteenth year of Josiah [the last good king] until some years beyond the captivity, the last 40 years before the destruction of Jerusalem in 586 B. C. Although Jeremiah was persecuted and imprisoned with brief periods of freedom, I divinely protected him and he continued as My messenger. Jeremiah as My Prophet continually warned that that the temple would be destroyed, and he said that the temple, the law, and the covenant would not insure Judah against My judgment.

Jeremiah's heart was right with Me throughout all his trials of being rejected by family, neighbors, priest, prophets, friends, his King, and all the people. I found Jeremiah wholly acceptable, and he was My most worthy Prophet. Many children have suffered through serious and difficult times but few have ever shown more loyalty than he did. It is the heart of man that proves right with Me. All My children should learn and heed these trials and tribulations that My loved ones have gone through, because the lessons are true teachers of My call and plan of accepting My children for eternity.

My dear children these teachings may seem boring, but I am not boring! I am laying before all to see how I view men's hearts. I expect you to honor My efforts, and find your path of improvement to allow Me to honor you and reward you when your hearts desire meets My hearts desire. Search the scriptures, find the one that points our your problem and then We will seek "improvement of heart" together. NO HONEST

EFFORT WILL BE OVERLOOKED. Know that I am ready to help in all
your efforts to improve your heart for Me.

10 "And yet for all this her treacherous sister Judah <u>has not turned to Me
with her whole heart, but in pretense,</u>" says the LORD. Jere. 3:10

14 "Return, O backsliding children," says the LORD; "for <u>I am married to
you</u>. I will take you, one from a city and two from a family, and I will
bring you to Zion. 15 And I will give you shepherds <u>according to My
heart</u>* who will feed you with knowledge and understanding." Jere.
3:14,15

17 "At that time Jerusalem shall be called The Throne of the LORD, and
all the nations shall be gathered to it, to the name of the LORD, to
Jerusalem. <u>No more shall they follow the dictates of their evil hearts.</u>"
Jere. 3:17

4 "<u>Circumcise yourselves to the LORD</u>, And take away <u>the foreskins of
your hearts</u>, You men of Judah and inhabitants of Jerusalem, Lest My fury
come forth like fire, And burn so that no one can quench *it*, Because of
the evil of your doings." Jere. 4:4

14 "O Jerusalem, <u>wash your heart from wickedness</u>, That you may be
saved. How long shall your evil thoughts lodge within you?" Jere. 4:14

18 "Your ways and your doings Have procured these *things* for you. This
is your wickedness, Because it is bitter, <u>Because it reaches to your heart</u>."
Jere. 4:18

23 "But this people has <u>a defiant and rebellious heart</u>; They have revolt-
ed and departed. 24 <u>They do not say in their heart</u>, "Let us now fear the
LORD our God, Who gives rain, both the former and the latter, in its season. He reserves for us the appointed weeks of the harvest." Jere. 5:23,24

24 "Yet they did not obey or incline their ear, but <u>followed the counsels
and the dictates of their evil hearts</u>, and went backward and not forward."
Jere. 7:24

20 "But, O LORD of hosts, You who judge righteously, <u>Testing the mind</u> <u>and the heart</u>, Let me see Your vengeance on them, For to You I have revealed my cause." Jere. 11:20

10 "This evil people, who refuse to hear My words, who <u>follow the dic-</u> <u>tates of their hearts,</u> and walk after other gods to serve them and worship them, shall be just like this sash which is profitable for nothing." Jere. 13:10

16 "Your words were found, and I ate them, And <u>Your word was to me</u> <u>the joy and rejoicing of my heart</u>; For I am called by Your name, O LORD God of hosts." Jere 15:16

12 "And you have done worse than your fathers, for behold, <u>each one fol-</u> <u>lows the dictates of his own evil heart</u>, so that no one listens to Me." Jere. 16:12

5 "Thus says the LORD: '<u>Cursed *is* the man</u> who trusts in man And makes flesh his strength, <u>Whose heart departs from the LORD.</u>'" JERE. 17:5

10 "<u>I, the LORD, search the heart, I test the mind</u>, Even to give every man according to his ways, According to the fruit of his doings." Jere. 17:10

17"Yet <u>your eyes and your heart *are* for nothing but your covetousness,</u> For shedding innocent blood, And practicing oppression and violence." Jere 22:17

20 "The anger of the LORD will not turn back <u>until He has executed and</u> <u>performed the thoughts of His heart.* In the latter days you will under-</u> <u>stand it perfectly.</u>" Jere. 23:20

7 "Then <u>I will give them a heart to know Me</u>, that I *am* the LORD; and they shall be My people, and I will be their God, for they shall return to Me <u>with their whole heart.</u>" Jere. 24:7

12 "Then <u>you will call upon Me</u> and go and pray to Me, and I will listen

to you. [13] And you will seek Me and find *Me* <u>when you search for Me with all your heart</u>." Jere. 29:12,13

[23] "Behold, the whirlwind of the LORD—Goes forth with fury, continuing whirlwind; It will fall violently on the head of the wicked. [24] The fierce anger of the LORD will not return until He has done it, And <u>until He has performed the intents of His heart.*</u> <u>In the latter days</u> you will consider it." Jere 30:23,24

[39] "Then <u>I will give them one heart and one way</u>, that they may fear Me forever, for the good of them and their children after them. [40] And I will make an everlasting covenant with them, that I will not turn away from doing them good; but <u>I will put My fear in their hearts</u> so that they will not depart from Me. [41] Yes, I will rejoice over them to do them good, and I will assuredly plant them in this land, <u>with all My heart* and with all My soul.</u>" Jere. 32:39-41

[29] "We have heard the pride of Moab   (He *is* exceedingly proud), Of his loftiness and arrogance and pride,   <u>And of the haughtiness of his heart.</u>" Jere. 48:29

*Note carefully the few times the Lord says things <u>about His heart,</u> remember this book is basically <u>about man's heart and God's heart.</u> There are only a few verses in the Bible <u>that speak of God's heart</u>, so it would seem important that His children should pay close attention to them.

Again note the few times God gives us a warning how He searches the <u>heart and the mind</u>. The heart, spoken of here, is our born-again new Spirit part, and the mind is the soul part [the soul is the mind, will, emotions, and the ego] that requires salvation so much. Our soul needs to depart completely from the guidance of the "Self", and submit completely to the obedience of the Holy Spirit. This teaching of the "self" in the Bible isn't highlighted enough as self, it is spoken of as "the flesh" or the "carnally minded." You are "in the Spirit" if indeed the Spirit of God dwells in you, but you are in the flesh of you are following the self.

EZEKIEL

Ezekiel was rare among My prophets in that <u>he was always staying close to My heart*</u> with and for Israel. He had a compassion for his people and closeness with the nation. His time was spent with the nation in its captivity and he more than any other prophet gave his testimony as "Thus says the Lord God." I gave him visions of heaven and of visions of prophecy like I gave no other prophet. The thrust of His prophesies showed his concern for Israel's future. <u>His heart for Me and for My Israel</u> made him the best prophet to release the coming victories of Israel with <u>their new heart</u>,* and with their becoming one nation upon the mountains of Israel forever. Ezekiel"s prophecies of the latter years stands out as a yet to be fulfilled ones, but many other ones have already come to pass. <u>Ezekiel's heart for Me was always acceptable</u> and We had many times together that <u>blessed My heart</u>. Ezekiel, as much as any other prophet, gave support to the necessity of My Lordship. I put My Spirit in Ezekiel, and sent him to the children of Israel. Eze. 2:2,3. I sent him there because Israel was <u>impudent, and hard-hearted</u>. Eze. 3:7. I said to him, receive into your heart all My words that I speak to you. Eze. 3:10. *God's heart

It was through Ezekiel that I instructed Israel that I would gather them from the countries where I scattered them, and give them the land of Israel, and I will <u>give them one heart and a new Spirit</u>. <u>I promised them if their hearts walk after the heart of detestable things</u> I would recompense their deeds. Eze. 11:17-21. I gave warnings about their <u>setting up idols in theirs heart</u>, and about having a <u>degenerate hearts</u>. <u>My concern was forever about the heart of Israel</u>. See also: Eze. 18:30-32, Eze. 33:31.

DANIEL

Daniel, who like Ezekiel was a captive in Babylon, was a child of Mine who <u>purposed in his heart</u> to do right, and I gave him favor and goodwill with the chief of eunuchs. Dan. 1:8,9. I was with Daniel watching him and guiding him because <u>his heart was right with My heart</u>. I used Daniel for many purposes but mainly to give comfort and to watch over My children in captivity. Daniel was used by Me <u>to teach the king about his heart</u>, and <u>who was really his God</u>. Dan. 2:30. My lesson for the King Nebuchadnezzar was for him to have proper appreciation for man's heart.

I let him have a change of heart from a man's heart to an animal's heart. Dan. 4:16. Just as this book teaches My children about their heart so I taught others before this time about hearts. I was bringing man's awareness to know <u>the Most High rules</u> in the Kingdom of man. Dan. 4:17.

My lesson for Nebuchadnezzar, <u>about his heart</u>, was made apparent to his son Belshazzar and to all peoples, nations, and languages that trembled and feared before him. Dan.5:18-22. The heart of King Darius was of My concern and I used the story of Daniel in the lion's den <u>to turn his heart to Daniel</u>. Dan 6:14. Daniel was a man after My own heart and he knew when to keep things just <u>in his own heart</u>. Dan. 7:28. I showed Daniel a great vision of things that must come because he <u>set his heart</u> to understand and to humble himself before Me. Dan. 10:12.

My dear children keep in your mind at all times that <u>I am always looking to the heart of My children</u>, and I am using this book to show you that I change not, these stories here shown are only to emphasis this act, and to bring you to the place that <u>you desire to change your heart</u> to meet My desires. Read your Bible in conjunction with reading this book, because then I can help you relate the Bible experiences to your own. We are in this growing time together so bring Me into all of your lessons.

HOSEA, JOEL AND AMOS

Hosea, Joel and Amos were each a prophet I called into My service to deal with My rebellious Judah and Israel. My people ceased from obeying Me because harlotry, wine and new wine <u>enslaved their hearts</u>. Hosea 4:11. Also the same with Joel and Amos, they were dealing with a rebellious people and all of My pleadings came to naught. They, My people, did not cry out to Me with <u>their heart</u>. Hosea 7:14. Their backsliding made My heart churn within Me and My sympathy was stirred. [Note, this is <u>God's heart</u> responding.] Hosea 11;8. They did not cry out to Me with <u>their hearts and their hearts were divided </u>and I held them guilty. Hosea 10 :2.

"Although I said, 'Turn to Me with all <u>your heart</u>, with fasting, and weeping,' still they would not listen to My prophets." Joel 2;12,13. I gave Amos warnings, visions of Locusts, Fire, the Plumb Line, and Summer

Fruit, in the end I still promised to raise them up even when <u>their hearts were far from Me.</u> Amos Chapters 7 and 8.

MINOR PROPHETS

There were few heart lessons to be learned during the times of the Minor Prophets until Malachi brought forth:

[1] "For behold, the day is coming, Burning like an oven, And all <u>the proud,</u> yes, all who <u>do wickedly</u> will be stubble. And the day which is coming shall burn them up," Says the LORD of hosts, "That will leave them neither root nor branch. [2] But to you who fear My name The <u>Sun of Righteousness</u> shall arise With healing in His wings; And you shall go out And grow fat like stall-fed calves. [3]You shall trample the wicked, For they shall be ashes under the soles of your feet On the day that I do *this,* Says the LORD of hosts." Malachi 4:1-3

Malachi brought the heralding cry announcing the soon coming of the Savior of the children of God, <u>the One who can make right the children's hearts.</u>

PAUSE AND REFLECT

ALL THROUGH THE OLD TESTAMENT GOD'S CONCERN FOR THE HEART OF MAN IS NEVER FAILING, AND IT IS SO PRECIOUS TO READ HOW GOD'S HEART WAS AFFECTED WITH MAN'S SUCCESSES AND FAILURES. DO NOT MISS THE IMPORTANCE OF THIS STUDY OF OLD TESTAMENT SAINT'S AND SINNER'S HEARTS. THIS IS THE PLACE GOD HAS GIVEN YOU THIS LESSON OVER AND OVER AGAIN. IT IS QUITE APPARENT MAN'S HEART HAS BEEN THE SAME SINCE THE FIRST MAN ADAM CAME ON THE SCENE. YOU AND ADAM HAVE THE SAME SPIRIT, BODY, AND SOUL TO CONTEND WITH. WHY SHOULD THIS LOOK THROUGH THE BIBLE AT THE HEART BE SO IMPORTANT AT THIS TIME? IT IS OF THE UTMOST IMPORTANCE NOW, MORE THAN EVER,

BECAUSE GOD'S CHILDREN SHOULD REALIZE THE TIME THEY NOW LIVE IN, AND HOW CLOSE THEY ARE TO THEIR RAPTURE. THEY ARE ABOUT TO BE CAUGHT UP IN THE SECOND MASS EXODUS OF MAN TO GOD'S HEAVEN. THE PREPARATION OF YOUR HEART MUST BE COMPLETED.

CHAPTER FOUR

2000 YEARS JESUS TO ARMAGEDDON ISRAEL PUT ON HOLD AND THE BRIDE BROUGHT FORTH

From Adam on God has been weaving a pattern of love to capture men's heart and bring them back to Him. First men were left on their own; this was a massive failure because there were found only a few men with right hearts. Then in the Old Testament Moses brought the Law, and no man was saved by the law, only sin was exposed by it, and man was shown how far he was from God's heart. Now God's Son was sent into earth to prepare the way for fallen man to come to God. Only by Jesus' death on the cross, and descend into hell to bear the whole of God's wrath on the sin of man, could this sacrifice make a way for man to come to God.

With the way now opened for man to come to God, man needed help to make the transition from flesh into the Spirit. It took 4000 years to bring man to a position that God could provide positive re-entry back into the Spirit realm from which he came. [Remember God breathed into his nostrils the breath of life.] Now you must understand no man had ever gone to heaven from earth, until Jesus returned to heaven, but Jesus didn't return to heaven alone. John 3:13.

THE FIRST RAPTURE

After Jesus' resurrection He led captivity [all men and women in Abraham's Bosom] captive.

8 "Therefore He says: *'When He ascended on high, <u>He led captivity captive</u> And gave gifts to men.'* 9 (Now this, *"He ascended"*—what does it mean but that He also first descended into the lower parts of the earth? 10 He who descended is also <u>the One who ascended far above all the heavens</u>, that He might fill all things.)" Eph.. 4; 8-10.

2 "I know a man in Christ who fourteen years ago—whether in the body I do not know, or whether out of the body I do not know, God knows—such a one was caught up to the third heaven. 3 And I know such a man—whether in the body or out of the body I do not know, God knows— 4 how <u>he was caught up into Paradise</u> and heard inexpressible words, which it is not lawful for a man to utter." 2 Cor. 12:2-4

Jesus took the Old Testament elect to their New Paradise, to a special place prepared by God, a part of God's place that surrounded God's City in Heaven. This was again a temporary place of waiting, only a more comfortable one. Remember they came from a place of holding in Death [Lu. 16:22,23, & 23:43] and they were to be kept apart until after the tribulation period was completed on earth. This remnant of Israel would only be given their Eternal Spirit bodies after the Judgment by Jesus in Israel just after His return to earth in Glory, His Second Coming.

Note, this is <u>The First Rapture</u>,* or catching away, of a large group of God's children. Thousands and thousands of them from Abraham's time to Jesus' time. This was God rescuing His First wife. Remember Enoch and Elijah weren't carried to heaven where God dwelled, but they were taken to a "Heavenly Place" God made for them in earth. The reason for this is God didn't own these people they were Satan's possessions, because Adam's sin gave the earth and all that's in it to him. If God took them at that time God would be violating His own decree. Not until Jesus' resurrection was Satan defeated, and then God could take men from earth!

In addition to Abraham's Bosom, Jesus took those who came out of the tombs at His resurrection to Heaven as a "First Fruits offering to God the Father" these were the first men raised after Jesus' resurrection. With Jesus' return to Heaven He was bringing a great host of Old Testament men and women to the new Paradise in Heaven. The term Rapture* means "the state of being carried away with joy, love, and pleasure, resulting in ecstasy."

50 "And Jesus cried out again with a loud voice, and yielded up His spirit. 51 Then, behold, the veil of the temple was torn in two from top to bottom; and the earth quaked, and the rocks were split, 52 and the graves were opened; and many bodies of <u>the saints who had fallen asleep</u> were raised; 53 and <u>coming out of the graves after His resurrection</u>, they went into the holy city and appeared to many." Matt. 27: 50-53.

20 "But now Christ is raised from the dead, *and* has become the first fruits of those who have fallen asleep. 21 For since by man *came* death, by Man also *came* the resurrection of the dead. 22 For as in Adam all die, even so in Christ all shall be made alive. 23 But each one in his own order: Christ the first fruits, afterward those *who are* Christ's at His coming." 1 Cor. 15:20-23.

THE HOLY SPIRIT
THE FIRST MAN RISING
IS THE HOLY SPIRIT

<u>This First Man Rising was God, wholly God, The Holy Spirit</u> willingly entering into the heart of man to abide there forever. With <u>this gift to the heart of man,</u> man would be able to be led into the path God set to bring him, properly equipped, into his Eternal Life. God had plans for this entry of man into Eternity, which would entail a three-stage move of God into man's heart, so man's born-again new Spirit would become fully "In His Image and Likeness! <u>The Holy Spirit was God's FIRST eternal gift of Himself to man after Jesus' sacrifice.</u>

To make a time break in the Bible you might agree that Israel's time ended when the Gospel of John closed and the Book of Acts started, and their Temple was finally destroyed about 40 years later, ending all sacrifices. The time of the Gentiles, with the forming of the Bride of Christ, was the great change for <u>God seeking man's heart</u>. Israel, as a nation, was scattered and <u>This First Man Rising was God, wholly God, The Holy Spirit</u> willingly entering into the heart of man to abide there forever. With <u>this gift to the heart of man</u>, man would be able to be led into the path God set to bring him, properly equipped, into his Eternal Life. God had plans for this entry of man into Eternity, which would entail a three-stage move of God into man's heart, so man's born-again new Spirit would become fully "In His Image and Likeness! <u>The Holy Spirit was God's **FIRST** eternal gift of Himself to man after Jesus' sacrifice.</u>

<u>God seeking man's heart was opened to all men</u> everywhere. This is a possible meaning of Jesus when He said "But many who are first [Israel] will be last, and the last [The Gentiles or Church] first." Mk. 10:31. You might say Israel was "put on hold" for this new move of God.

This time was set as truly different because Jesus said to His disciples "I will pray the Father, and He will give you another helper, that He may abide with you forever, even the Spirit of Truth, whom the world cannot receive, because it neither sees Him nor knows Him; but you know Him for He dwells with you and will be in you." John 14:16,17. This is a brand new plan to bring man to God, not used any time before. God's new plan for the return of man to God's Heaven was now the **"FIRST MAN RISING."** The first permanent entry of God into the flesh body of lost man was to put a helper inside him <u>who will bring lost man's heart wholly back to God</u>.

The New Testament reveals man's new way of exercising God's gift of Himself, by <u>the renewing of the heart of man</u> to become a Son of God. Now look again into scripture to see how God closed out His time with Israel. In the four Gospels God told the Jews how they should act [such as the beatitudes] but they weren't given the gift of the Holy Spirit to help and guide them, that was given only to the new born-again followers of Jesus after Jesus' ascension. Just as Israel was given 2000 years, [Abraham to Jesus] so is God giving the church 2000 years. [Jesus to the

Rapture and the beginning of the tribulation, the time of Jacob's trouble]
The seven years of Tribulation are the last years reserved for completing
God's work with the Nation of Israel prior to giving them a new heart.

24 "For I will take you from among the nations, gather you out of all
countries, and bring you into your own land. 25 Then I will sprinkle clean
water on you, and you shall be clean; I will cleanse you from all your
filthiness and from all your idols. 26 I will give you a new heart and put
a new spirit within you; I will take the heart of stone out of your flesh and
give you a heart of flesh. 27 I will put My Spirit within you and cause you
to walk in My statutes, and you will keep My judgments and do *them.*"
Eze. 36:24-27.

Now with Jesus in heaven the last words He spoke to His eleven disciples
still rang in their ears, "Go into all the world and preach and publish the
good news [The Gospel] to every creature." Mk. 16:14,15. They were
told to go and wait for what the Father had promised, "You shall receive
power when the Holy Spirit has come upon you." Acts 1:4-8. They obe-
diently gathered together in prayer while waiting for the baptism of the
Holy Spirit. When that day had fully come, "Suddenly there came a sound
from heaven, a violent trumpet blast, and they were all, about 120, filled
with the Holy Spirit and all began to speak in different languages." [or
tongues] Acts 2:2-4.

This event was the basic start of God's move on men to put the Holy
Spirit into man and change man's heart, only by God indwelling man can
man be brought into the Spirit realm of God. This same mission of God,
started with the 12 apostles, has never changed, that is to bring lost men
into their salvation by receiving Jesus in their heart as their Savior, and
then further empowering them by receiving the baptism of the Holy
Spirit. All men born-again have the Holy Spirit, but with the Baptism they
receive His power and have a release for the Spiritual Gifts to flow.

JESUS ON EARTH
MEN'S HEARTS IN JESUS' TIME

In speaking to the children of Israel Jesus was saying, "Blessed are the pure in heart for they shall see God," and He also said , "Whoever looks at a women to lust for her has already committed adultery with her in his heart, for where your treasure is, there is you heart also." Matt. 5:8,28; 6:21. Jesus brought to mankind, through the children of Israel, clear truth that showed men what and where their major problem was, it was a heart problem. This was what was keeping them from a closer walk with God. Making it a clear "heart problem" was the blessing Jesus was giving first to the tribes of Israel. He said He was meek and lowly in heart and out of man's mouth the heart speaks. Matt. 11:29; 12:34. Here was a revealed message that the heart needed a change or renewing for man's mouth to speak bringing forth good treasure, the first real lesson in acting like God. How was man to bring all of the change about that God said he needed? Not in their own strength, but only through God, could this change of heart come about. Jesus said, "Their heart is far from Me," and out of their heart proceeds evil thoughts, murders, adulteries, fornications, thefts, false witness, and blasphemies. What must a man do? Matt. 15:8,18,19; Mk. 16:14. So Jesus told them, "To love the Lord your God with all your heart, all your soul, and with all your mind, and love you neighbor as yourself." Matt 22:37-39. Jesus was putting all of man's correction on man to do it himself and no man could bring his heart to the perfection God required. All of Jesus' help for Israel always came back to man doing the heart change God required through his own strength, but Jesus knew it wasn't Israel's time.

As you have seen in this book, all through the Old Testament God was dealing with man's heart from Adam on. Many were saved because of God's love for them and their love for God, but their hearts still needed a change. In the four Gospels the same things occurred in men's heart as they had from the beginning, but before Jesus left His disciples His last move to help them was when He breathed on them and said receive the Holy Spirit. This was the first release of the Holy Spirit into men in permanent residence. The disciples were the first men to be "Born-again," and then they were asked to terry until the Holy Spirit came upon them, and they were all filled with the Holy Spirit and began to speak with other tongues, exhibiting the "Baptism of the Holy Spirit." John 20:22; Acts 2;1-4.

JESUS IN HEAVEN
MEN'S HEARTS IN THE NEW TESTA-MENT TIME

As the disciples were spreading the good news with boldness, all the multitudes of those who believed were <u>of One Heart</u> and one soul, Acts 4:32. Now God the Holy Spirit was able to do what man alone could not, <u>change their heart to a heart of flesh</u> from those <u>stony hearts</u> they were before. The penalty of lying to the Holy Spirit [GOD] was made apparent to them when Ananias was taken in death at his attempted deception of the price of land he was selling. He was asked , "Why have you <u>conceived this thing in your Heart?</u>" This lesson was making quite clear this offense was against God <u>in their heart</u>! Acts 5:3,4

Many of God's children were martyred for their belief in God, Stephen was the first of the disciples put to this test. It was Stephen telling the council and high priest that they were <u>stiff-necked and uncircumcised in heart</u> and ears that caused him to be stoned. Acts 7:51 In Samaria the Apostles told <u>Simon that his heart was not right</u> in God's sight and he should repent and pray that God would forgive him. Acts 8:21,22. On the road to Gaza Phillip was instructing a eunuch from Ethiopia how to receive Jesus when he said, "<u>If you believe with all your heart</u> you may receive Him." Acts 8:37. Barnabas and Saul at Antioch found men there that the hand of the Lord was with them so they encouraged them all, that <u>with purpose of heart</u> they should continue with the Lord. Acts 11:23.

During Paul's ministry in Rome he was teaching the leaders of the Jews about the Kingdom of God and Jesus, and some were persuaded and some disbelieved. So when they did not agree The Holy Spirit spoke rightly through Isaiah, and Paul quoted from Isaiah 6:8-10, telling them <u>their heart has grown dull</u>, and they should <u>understand with their heart</u> and return and be healed. In Paul's Epistle to the Romans he wrote, "Although men knew God they did not Glorify Him as God, nor were they thankful, but became futile in their thoughts, and foolish hearts were darkened." Rom. 1:21. Paul was saying only the Holy Spirit can bring the things of God to man, only by bringing truth to man's heart, then his head will learn. Paul also said with your hardness and impenitent heart you are treasuring up for yourselves wrath in the day of wrath and revelation of the righteous Judgment of God. Rom. 2:5. One of Paul's statements that rings so true today was "The word is near you, even in your mouths and in your heart, that if you confess with your mouth the Lord Jesus and believe in your heart that God has raised Him from the dead, you will be saved. For with the heart one believes to righteousness and with the mouth confession is made to salvation. Rom. 10:8-10

Paul was teaching, "Eye has not seen, nor ear heard, nor have entered into the heart of man the things which God has prepared for those who love Him." I Cor. 2:9. Paul was saying only the Holy Spirit can bring the things of God to man, only by bringing truth to man's heart, then his head will learn. Paul teaches how men should treat a wife or a virgin, saying he who stands steadfast in his heart having no necessity, but has power over his own will, and has determined in his heart that he will keep his virgin, does well. I Cor. 7:37. Again teaching that man should have a close watch over his own heart in everything! Paul also makes a strong case for the Holy Spirit revealing the secrets of the heart. 1 Cor. 14:25.

Paul points out from scripture even to his day a veil lies over the hearts of the children of Israel. 2 Cor. 3:15. Paul, speaking of the Gentiles, says they walk with futility of their mind because of the hardening of their hearts. Eph. 4:17,18. Also in Ephesians Paul speaks of the joy of the Spirit and singing and making melody in your heart to the Lord. Eph. 5:18,19. Paul told servants, be obedient to those who are your masters [or bosses] according to the flesh, with fear and trembling, in sincerity of heart, as to Christ; not with eye service, as men-pleasers, but as servants of Christ, doing the will of God from the heart. Eph. 6:5,6. Paul said one should love from a pure heart, from a good conscience, and from sincere faith. I Tim. 1:5. God was angry with his children because they went astray in their heart. Heb. 3:10. Do not be carried about with various and strange doctrines. For it is good that the heart be established with grace. Heb. 13:9.

If anyone among you thinks he is religious, and does not bridle his tongue but <u>deceives his own heart</u>, this one's religion is useless. James 1: 26. Learn to love one another fervently <u>with a pure heart</u>. I Peter 1 :22. In I Peter 3:3,4, do not let your outward beauty be that outward kind of "hair, clothes, and gold" but let it be the <u>HIDDEN PERSON OF THE HEART</u>, which is very precious in the sight of God. Do not have eyes full of adultery and cannot cease from sin, who are beguiling and unstable souls. They have <u>a heart trained in covetous practices</u>, and ARE ACCURSED CHILDREN. 2 Peter 2: 13,14 If our <u>heart condemns</u> us, God is greater than our heart, and knows all things. Beloved if our heart <u>does not condemn</u> us, we have confidence toward God. I John 3:20,21. The last word in the Bible about hearts speaks only about Babylon, she says in her heart, "I sit as queen and am no widow, and will not sorrow. <u>How terrible is deception in the heart</u>! Rev. 18:7,8.

CHURCH HISTORY

This chapter has walked through the Bible from Jesus' time until the present time, looking carefully for the things concerning men's heart. With that as background consider where God's heart is in these present days. Our Heavenly Father has watched over the Church [This is the Church's age and time.] and He knows just where all men's hearts are. These twenty centuries have buried all men from Jesus to the present ones living now. Did the Gospels save men through these centuries? The answer is yes, but were there enough saved? Probably not.

What are We, who are alive today, going to do to fill out God's heart's desire for a family? Just before us is the end of the church age, and no more children will ever come into heaven as the "Bride of Christ," after we are caught up in the church rapture. Shouldn't we be spreading the gospel with all our ability right now to give Our precious Heavenly Father His complete family? Shouldn't we be giving Our precious Jesus His full Bride? Now don't say won't they be receiving more people all through the Tribulation and be adding souls for the next 1000 years. Yes that is all true, but those are not part of the Bride of Christ! There is a special love and desire in Jesus' and the Father's heart for those who come to them during the church age, and we who are alive in the very end of this time should be spreading "The Word" with all of our abilities!

This book will make clear the groups of men that will be saved and the ones who are lost, but right now is the place to make this plea to you who are reading this, don't you know these times and the heart of God for Jesus' Bride? Come and be a witness for Christ each day, showing your love for Him through answering the call He puts in your heart at this time.

This end of the church age is covering the earth with the gospel truth like no other time, ever! Christian television has finally covered the major and most minor areas of the earth with the greatest array of Apostles, Prophets, Pastors, Teachers and Evangelists ever imagined. Radio has done this service since its inception and still continues to do so. Why would this coverage be so complete at this time? THIS IS THE LAST OF THIS AGE! Just before all who are alive in these times is the blessing of the "Catching Away" of God's church, Jesus' Bride. ARE you who ARE HIS ready and bringing all who you are able to bring into this gift from God to His Son Jesus?

PREPARATIONS BEFORE THE CATCHING AWAY

Matthew 25:I-13 Believer's Study Bible

The initial parable employs the pageantry of an Oriental wedding. Several observations will aid in the understanding of the parable. Eastern weddings were set for a given day, but Orientals have never been as bound by precision of starting or ending times as are those in western culture. The bridal party was to be ready. Sometime after sundown, members of the groom's party, bearing lamps on poles, would depart from the home of the groom and proceed through the streets in a gala procession. They would join with the bridal party, and the two would wind back through the village to the place designated for the ceremony and the wedding feast. The ten virgins of the parable are part of the bridal party. Five realize that a time lapse could occur and come prepared for any exigency. Five are foolish (*mougrai*, Gk.) and consequently unprepared. The application by Jesus is that men must continuously be prepared and watching if they wish to enter the kingdom when the King comes.

This parable is pertaining to the position of the church before the catching away. It is using "Oil" as a foundation of the story. Oil in scriptures says oil is for light, or enlightenment. Exo. 25:6. In studying this tale told by Jesus we discover that 5 virgins are permitted to enter the marriage chamber with the bridegroom, but 5 are not allowed, the bridegroom says to them I do not know you. Scripture is saying some children are not ready for the "Rapture". Another example of Christians [Or so called Christians] is given.

15 "I know your works, that you are neither cold nor hot. I could wish you were cold or hot. 16 So then, because you are lukewarm, and neither cold nor hot, I will vomit you out of My mouth. 17 Because you say, 'I am rich, have become wealthy, and have need of nothing—and do not know that you are wretched, miserable, poor, blind, and naked.'" Rev. 3:15-17

These two examples are saying don't be ignorant or lukewarm or you will miss this wonderful blessing as the Bride of Christ. This book is encouraging all who belong to Christ or come to Him eager and willing to learn truth. Be a doer not just a reader of the word. The virgin story is about 5 virgins who were prepared or were ready, Matt. 25:10. See that you are ready; you've studied, believed, and are doing the work given to you by your Heavenly Father, you are working His plan for you.

Foot note: This story above leaves a question will the 5 foolish virgins be lost forever or will they have an opportunity to be saved? They do not become part of the Bride, but yes they will have three more chances, but it will be under most difficult circumstances. They will have to go through the Tribulation. They may be killed, or beheaded, for their testimony of Jesus. They may hang onto the robes of a Jew, Zech. 8:23, to be saved and go up in the third rapture, mid-trib, Rev. 7:9. They may believe the two witnesses or the testimony of God's three angels and be saved and live through the tribulation or be killed for their testimony. None of these options should encourage anyone to not be prepared now!

Here is a good place to bring up how to do it! How to do what? Why how to be prepared and ready for Jesus to sound that Trumpet, so read carefully!

One of the purposes of the "Glory Series" of books [12 of them with follow ons] is to aid in the Bride's Physical and Spiritual growth. The body is the temple of the living God; just what kind of body would you want Him to dwell in? To be made ready is to be prepared in every area that is to belong to Jesus. It should be the work of the preparing Christian to take proper care of the physical body by eating the proper foods. Deuteronomy 14:1-21 shows God's concern for Israel's eating habits, shouldn't the Bride be as concerned about what they eat? There are many up to date Christian books regarding the eating of proper foods that are now available for the study and practice of good eating habits. In the same way of taking care of the physical body, exercise and correct body training should be encouraged for a loving believing Bride.

Here are seven suggestions for a renewal of your pattern of living.

One, Drink at least 8-10 glasses of pure filtered water daily, not tap water!
Two, Get a full night's sleep. Learn to find the rest God provides.
Three, Seek freedom from stress, enjoy more laughter and joyful times.
Four, Choose "living foods" eat more fresh fruit and vegetables.
Five, Sustain a regular exercise program.
Six, Plan a regular "Detoxification Program," by fasting.
Seven, Take true, natural, multi-vitamins and mineral supplements. See 1 Cor. 9:27, "I discipline my body."

These are quick, simple, and brief thoughts about your work of preparation so you will appear before Jesus as an eager willing Bride. What you do and how much you do will basically depend on <u>what your heart's desire is</u> as the potential Bride of Christ. Never doubt your victory, never be anxious for anything but in all things believe and be led by the Holy Spirit, for He will never fail you or leave you behind. Make every effort to draw closer in your daily walk knowing to whom you belong.

The primary way of preparation requires constant contact with God through the Hoy Spirit. When communication is established and is regular, early every morning, then the growing becomes the obeying of the path set by your Holy Spirit. This is the way of Spiritual Growth. The waiting Church should become overcoming conquerors, moving in power, love, and a sound mind able to pull down strongholds of the enemy. The working, growing church should be watching and praying, and giving the opposition his just dues in every case.

The Church should be eagerly looking for Jesus' return in the air. Heb. 9:28 says, "Unto them that look for Him shall He appear the second time." Titus 2:13 says, "The church should be looking for that blessed hope and the glorious appearing of the Great God and our Savior Jesus Christ. When the word says look, watch, and looking, they all mean that <u>the waiting Bride is to be eagerly anticipating an event with preparation.</u> The implication is strongly made to make a commitment, and dedication with alertness. All of this should make clear the Church, the body of Christ on earth, should never fail to watch, pray, and hopefully anticipate the appearing of Jesus in the clouds.

I beseech you therefore, brethren, by the mercies of God, that you <u>present your bodies</u> a living sacrifice, holy, acceptable to God, *which is* your reasonable service. 2 "And do not be conformed to this world, but <u>be transformed by the renewing of your mind</u>, that you may prove what *is* that good and acceptable and perfect will of God. 3 For I say, through the grace given to me, to everyone who is among you, not to think *of himself* more highly than he ought to think, but to think soberly, as God has dealt to each one a measure of faith. 4 For as we have many members in one body, but all the members do not have the same function, 5 so we, *being* many, are one body in Christ, and individually members of one another.

6 Having then gifts differing according to the grace that is given to us, *let us use them:* if prophecy, *let us prophesy* in proportion to our faith; 7 or ministry, *let us use it* in *our* ministering; he who teaches, in teaching; 8 he who exhorts, in exhortation; he who gives, with liberality; he who leads, with diligence; he who shows mercy, with cheerfulness. 9 *Let* love *be* without hypocrisy. Abhor what is evil. Cling to what is good. 10 *Be* kindly affectionate to one another with brotherly love, in honor giving preference to one another; 11 not lagging in diligence, fervent in spirit, serving the Lord; 12 rejoicing in hope, patient in tribulation, continuing steadfastly in prayer; 13 distributing to the needs of the saints, given to hospitality. Rom." 12:1-13

Carefully note this word given in Romans 12:1,2. These verses bring out a need as important as the requirement to be born again, it says to make a <u>dedication of our Soul [Mind] and our Body</u>.

23 "Now may the God of peace Himself sanctify you completely; and <u>may your whole spirit, soul, and body </u>be preserved blameless at the coming of our Lord Jesus Christ. 24 He who calls you *is* faithful, who also will do *it*." 1 Thess. 5:23,24

God's desire is that His children <u>belong wholly to Him.</u> You should have by now accepted Jesus in your heart, but that isn't your whole person, you still should also <u>dedicate your mind and body to Him with your whole heart</u> just as you did with your heart [Your Spirit]. will you take the time right now to do just that? This seems to be something that is not taught as much as it should be. My dear children have no doubt about the times you are presently in, these are the last, <u>the very last</u>, days of this Church age. You who are His know that soon, very soon, Jesus will come to call us who belong to Him to meet Him in the air, and so will we be with Him forevermore.

THE SECOND RAPTURE

Where is that in the Bible? Here are some verses that provoke positive thoughts along the line of God's heart's desire for His children. It is not the purpose of this book to dwell on any particular area of scripture in great depth so if you desire more detail of this subject read each reference given below. God wanted salvation for Noah and his family. Gen. 7:1. God wanted Lot and family saved. Gen. 19:15,16. God wanted Godly people saved. Other verses that indicate <u>where God's heart is</u> on this subject: Lu. 21:36, John 14:3, Rom. 5:9, 1 Cor 15:51-55, 2 Cor. 4:14, Eph. 5:6, 1 Thess. 1:10, 1 Thess. 4:13-17, 1 Thess. 5:9, 2 Thess. 2:1, Heb. 9:28, 2 Pet. 2:5,7,9. and Rev. 3:10. No scripture says the word Rapture, but these two verses are speaking to this "Catching Away": Psalm 12:1 and 1 Thess.4:13-18.

Psalm 12:1

David was given this verse by the Holy Spirit to start a Psalm; however the verse just doesn't seem to connect to anything that follows. Was God really that eager to tell his children how much He desired them to be with

Him that He put this little note in this place? This is the very first time a catching away or disappearance of a number of men is indicated.
Help, LORD, for the godly man ceases! For the faithful disappear from among the sons of men. [New King James Bible]

Help, Lord! For principled Godly people are here no more; faithful vanish from among the sons of men. [Amplified Bible]

This is just the scene expected after the "Catching Away" or Rapture. The men left on earth will be searching for all the men and women who were known to be principled and Godly people. They will say where have all the faithful vanished or disappeared? Another scripture that gives explanation to how that miracle will happen is:

1 Thessalonians 4:13-18
The Comfort of Christ's Coming

13 "But I do not want you to be ignorant, brethren, concerning those who have fallen asleep, lest you sorrow as others who have no hope. 14 For if we believe that Jesus died and rose again, even so God will bring with Him those who sleep in Jesus. 15 For this we say to you by the word of the Lord, that we who are alive *and* remain until the coming of the Lord will by no means precede those who are asleep. 16 For the Lord Himself will descend from heaven with a shout, with the voice of an archangel, and <u>with the trumpet of God</u>. And the dead in Christ will rise first. 17 Then we who are alive *and* remain shall be caught up together with them in the clouds to meet the Lord in the air. And thus we shall always be with the Lord. 18 Therefore comfort one another with these words."

Jesus will be coming from God's Heaven to Earth and this scripture indicates that He will bring with Him all of those children of God who previously have died and gone to be with Jesus in Heaven, this is what it means by "those who are asleep, or the dead in Christ will rise first." [Note, it says those who are asleep indicating they are "At rest in the Lord."] It is obvious that we who remain are the ones alive on earth at the time of Jesus' coming in the air. This simply put is the Rapture. At the end of the age of the gentiles, the Bridegroom will come for His Bride and take Her to God's Heaven. There He will present Her as the Church reflecting His own Glory, perfect without blemish, spot, or wrinkle, a Holy Bride suitable for a Holy Bridegroom. As the word indicates God has a rescue and recovery program. Jesus will come in the clouds above earth and meet His Bride in the air.

On Heaven's side of this meeting there is tremendous color and light, Love glowing, undulating, and moving in heavenly rhythm. The Glory of God flowing to Jesus and from Jesus to His Bride causing an unbelievable Beauty to fill all the Heavens. God's Heavenly Host are filling the skies waiting in great anticipation this never before seen extravagant exhibition of God's love displayed in such an far-reaching manner. The Joy, Love, and Happiness of the meeting in the clouds bring to sweet fulfillment God's plan for Jesus and His Bride, the Church. Each of the children will be caught from earth and from Heaven; to meet Jesus and see Him as He truly is, because they will be like Him. They are then in eternal bodies patterned after Jesus' own resurrected body!

Behold what manner of love the Father has bestowed on us, that we should be called children of God! Therefore the world does not know us, because it did not know Him. 2 "Beloved, now we are children of God; and it has not yet been revealed what we shall be, but we know that when He is revealed, <u>we shall be like Him, for we shall see Him as He is</u>. 3 And <u>everyone who has this hope in Him purifies himself, just as He is pure</u>." 1 John 3:1-3

It is important to take notice here about the love God has bestowed upon the Bride of Christ; <u>not in any other Rapture</u> does God make such a great heavenly spectacle of the Bride's meeting in the air. <u>The blessing of God's Glory flowing</u> to Jesus then to the Bride and back again is not mentioned at any other Rapture time.

3 "Blessed *be* the God and Father of our Lord Jesus Christ, who has <u>blessed us with every spiritual blessing in the heavenly *places* in Christ,</u> 4 just as He chose us in Him before the foundation of the world, that we should be holy and without blame <u>before Him in love</u>, 5 having predestined us to adoption as sons by Jesus Christ to Himself, according to the good pleasure of His will, 6 <u>to the praise of the glory of His grace, by which He made us accepted in the Beloved.</u>" Eph. 1:3-6.

"The elders who are among you I exhort, I who am a fellow elder and a witness of the sufferings of Christ, and <u>also a partaker of the glory</u> that will be revealed. [4] <u>and when the Chief Shepherd appears, you will receive the crown of glory</u> that does not fade away." 1 Peter 5:1,4

Another special blessing will be the meeting of family members who have previously died and gone to Heaven, what a wonderful happy victory there will be at this time. There will be love shown, shared, and observed, making everyone feel at home at last. This newness of Spiritual reality will stir and awaken everyone as this part of Heaven is revealed for all to share. The beautiful harmony of <u>God's Glory and Love</u> will be drawing everyone into this newness of Love's Glory revealed. The Joy and Love from the Father and the Son fills and refills the Bride. The new freedom of Spiritual cleansing has touched the entire Bride leaving everyone pure, chaste, undefiled, and guiltless.

There is released a sense of Oneness with Father God, and Jesus as never before possible. This occurs through the Holy Spirit's indwelling each one and by His release of all of God's desires for His children. A completely new sense of love and being alive is experienced through the joyousness of Oneness <u>and the flooding about of the warmth of the Glory of Jesus</u>. From this meeting in the clouds the Bride's next stop will be God's Heavenly Home and the judgment seat of Christ. Just when that occurs is not made clear but it will be before the Marriage Supper of the Lamb.

SEVEN-YEAR TRIBULATION

Occurring simultaneously with the Bride's time in Heaven

Israel's time of completion comes through the cleansing of past ways. Old beliefs holding God's First Wife in bondage must come to an open display of its worthlessness. The culmination of God's plan of redemption will only come as Jesus is brought forth to Israel as the Lamb of God exposed. Israel will be set up for <u>one last testing of their hearts</u>, will God be accepted in truth as Israel's belief is faced with Satan exposed?

The Father is <u>seeking Israel's true heart</u> to be shown, giving Him <u>His heart's desire</u>; Israel cleansed, healed, and saved. This time of Jacob's troubles, Jer. 30:7, will not find "all Israel saved," but only one-third will survive. Zech. 13:8 showing God's determination for cleansed hearts only! The Father calls out 144,000 bondservants of God and seals them upon their foreheads. 12,000 men out of each tribe of Israel who have not defiled themselves by having relations with women, for they are pure virgins who follow the Lamb wherever He goes. No lie was found on their lips for they are blameless before the throne of God [Their hearts are found right]. Rev. 14 :1-5.

In the first half of the seven years the work of salvation by the 144,000 chosen servants of God covers the nations of the earth as Satan works his plan. God finds <u>men with right hearts</u> when they are found holding onto the garments of God's faithful Jews. <u>Right hearts are saved</u> despite Satan's efforts to discourage the active saints, Zech. 8:23. During the last 3 1\2 years God sends three angels, having the everlasting gospel to teach to those dwelling on earth, to every nation, tribe, and tongue and people to find those whose <u>hearts are right</u> before God. Rev. 14:6-11. These angels also tell of God's wrath upon the unrepentant, unsaved, lost men of the earth <u>whose hearts sought to please only their "self."</u>

The seven years of Jacobs's troubles are basically God's work of cleansing the earth and the heavens of evil while reaping His harvest of "Acceptable Hearts." The loving kindness of God never fails to protect the saints and saved souls <u>with right hearts</u> before God, although many of the saved are killed for their faith. Rev. 12:11, 14:12, 20:4. Besides the three angels proclaiming salvation over the earth, God also set His two witnesses in Jerusalem who prophesy 1260 days, and they bring great destruction around the earth while spreading the saving news of the word of God. Rev. 11;3-6.

This destruction comes about <u>because of God's fallen angels and men's evil hearts and evil ways</u>. This is a necessary cleansing to set up the earth healed, cleansed, and acceptable for Jesus' 1000 year reign over Israel and the nations. There are still lessons for Israel and the nations to grow into <u>God's children of His heart</u>.

MORE RAPTURES

THE THIRD RAPTURE

God called for two Raptures during the Gentiles or Church's 2000 years, one occurred after Jesus' resurrection when He ascended in the air and took captivity captive, Abraham's Bosom, and the other will be when Jesus takes His Bribe from earth to Heaven in the clouds. There was one catching away at the beginning if the church age and there will be one at the end.

 Now it appears that God has planned three "Catching Aways" for Israel all during the Seven Year Tribulation, the time of Jacob's troubles. This third Rapture occurs at the mid-tribulation time when suddenly a great multitude which no one could number, of all nations, tribes, peoples and tongues were found standing before the throne of God and before the Lamb, thus showing the successful work of the 144,000 chosen men of Israel. Rev. 7:7-14. Note there are only two groups of people prominent now; the Jesus people are not spoken of except when they are killed for their testimony. They are then found beneath the Altar.

THE FOURTH RAPTURE

The next Rapture occurs when John says in Revelation Chapter 14, "I looked and behold a Lamb standing on Mount Zion in Heaven, and with Him 144,000 men who were <u>redeemed from the earth</u>. This was apparently God rewarding His faithful Jews for their good work of witnessing for the Lamb of God during the first half of the tribulation, or a little longer. God in His mercy takes them out of the worst times, the last half of the Great Tribulation. Rev. 14:1-3

THE FIFTH RAPTURE

One more Rapture occurs at the end of the seven years of tribulation when God removes His Two Witnesses from earth after their death and resurrection. They are viewed ascending to heaven in a cloud after hearing a loud voice call out "Come Up Here," all of their enemies saw them. Rev. 11;3-12

The remarkable thing about these last three raptures are they are not prophesied about or remarked about in any other scriptures, God just pulls His children out of the fire without any prior notice! Asking why would God do this leads to questioning just who all these people are. One obvious thing about all of these people is God loves them very much, and the second obvious assumption follows they all seem to be born-again; therefore it would follow they <u>all have hearts that love God</u>. This proves He is the same yesterday, today and forever because He has stated His love for His Israel over and over again. Didn't He say in Luke 21:34,36 that His children should keep awake and watch, praying they may have strength and ability to escape all these things?

THE BRIDE IN HEAVEN
SEVEN YEARS

ASSEMBLING OF THE ELDERS AND
THE CHURCH

The Church's first place of assembly will be as The Father directs the twelve chosen Disciples of Christ to their places of Honor on 12 of the 24 thrones about His Throne. They are seated as Elders in Heaven along with the twelve chosen Leaders of the Twelve Tribes of Israel, all who have been in Paradise in Heaven since the First Rapture. The Church, the Bride, or the Body of Christ, are represented by something <u>like a sea of glass</u> because they have the peace that passes understanding, the tranquility of Heaven has settled on them before the Throne of God. Rev. 4:2-6.

THE HEAVENLY HOMES

All of the Bride will unite again in God's Place. Those who were previously there through death will be able to show off the places of Paradise, God's City, God's Throne, and the beautiful areas surrounding God's

City. Great mountains, valleys, rivers, and forests that is round about giving spectacular views everywhere one looked. The family members will eagerly show off their mansion homes, and then take each one to his own place prepared for them by Jesus. What a happy, joyous time this will be.

THE HEAVENLY PEOPLE

There will be meetings with many of the Old Testament and New Testament Bible people, such as Abraham, King David, Paul of Tarsus, Peter and on and on there will be an endless array of God's people. The number of people is beyond comprehension, thus it is beyond the capability of everyone meeting each other until the proper time has been given. Attention will be spent with family and friends to start with; this will take up the time allotted.

THE HEAVENLY PLACE

When the Bride first arrives the impact of the size of God's Place will be astounding to everyone. Heaven is a huge place, a million miles in every direction. Space unbelievable, filled with beauty that only God could create for His Home. The only light comes from God Himself; there are no suns, moons or stars there. God's Heaven is beyond words to explain or describe, you must be there! God's home is a gigantic planet the exception is God's Heaven is inside not on the outside! The references are the following scriptures. Ps. 84:11,

1 "Great *is* the Lord, and greatly to be praised In the city of our God, *In* His holy mountain, Psalm 48:1,2 2 Beautiful in elevation, *Is* Mount Zion *on* the sides of the north, The city of the great King."

9 "He made the Bear, Orion, and the Pleiades, And the chambers of the south; 10 He does great things past finding out, Yes, wonders without number." Job 9:9,10

12 "How you are fallen from heaven, O Lucifer, son of the morning! *How* you are cut down to the ground, You who weakened the nations!Isa.

14:12-14 [13] For <u>you have said in your heart</u>: '<u>I will ascend into heaven,</u> <u>I will exalt my throne above the stars of God</u>;   <u>I will also sit on the</u> <u>mount of the congregation On the farthest sides of the north</u>; [14] I will ascend above the heights of the clouds, <u>I will be like the Most High</u>.'"

The explanations are as follows: Inside of the sphere of God's planet He, God, has placed <u>His great City on the northern sides</u> of the inside of the planet. This explains why there are no suns, moons, or stars. On the southern sides is the <u>Chambers of the South</u>, this is where His heavenly angels have their residence. How do I know this, I asked and He told me. It is this author's belief that the Bride of Jesus will not see or be able to view the Heavenly City of Jerusalem at this time because it will have left Heaven for the journey to earth for the following reasons. See Rev. 21:2

ONE, It would seem God should hold back The Bride's viewing of their "Heavenly New City of Jerusalem" until All of God's children have been gathered. Remember there is still 1000 years for God to fill out His prop-er number of loved ones. Why should some see it first before the rest have a chance? Also why would He tease "The Bride" with showing them the "New Jerusalem" then require to them wait 1000 years before they could live there?

<u>**TWO**</u>, God's place is 1000 light years from earth [A light year is 5 1\2 Trillion miles] and it will take the New Jerusalem 1000 years to travel through space at the speed of light to arrive and satellite Earth on God's schedule. There is just the 7 years ahead of us, plus a few, then the Bride returns with Jesus for His 1000 year reign on earth, after that God will bring the Holy City, the New Jerusalem, out of heaven to its near earth location in just the perfect time. The Great White Throne Judgment will be over, death will be defeated, the Lake of fire will have had its filling. The New Heavens and the New Earth will have been prepared, that is they will have been regenerated, refreshed and renewed by God.* Each will have been made ready for God's children to have their "Eternity Beginning," IN THE NEW HEAVENS AND THE NEW EARTH.

* 2 Peter 3:7

[7] "But the heavens and the earth *which* are now preserved by the same word, <u>are reserved for fire until the day of judgment</u> and perdition of ungodly men."

*2 Peter 3:10-13

10 "But the day of the Lord will come as a thief in the night, in which the heavens will pass away with a great noise, and the elements will melt with fervent heat; both the earth and the works that are in it will be burned up. 11 Therefore, since all these things will be dissolved, what manner *of persons* ought you to be in holy conduct and godliness, 12 looking for and hastening the coming of the day of God, because of which the heavens will be dissolved, being on fire, and the elements will melt with fervent heat? 13 Nevertheless we, according to His promise, look for <u>new heavens</u> and a <u>new earth</u> in which righteousness dwells."

* Isaiah 66:22.

22 "'For as the <u>new heavens</u> and the <u>new earth</u> which I will make shall remain before Me," says the LORD, "So shall your descendants and your name remain.'"

"New" in Greek is Kainos = in freshness from the prime word Neoteros = of things, <u>regenerate</u>. "New" in Hebrew the prime root is Chadash = to be new, <u>rebuild, renew or repair</u>. This author believes it is foolish to assume God would ever totally destroy Earth or the Heavens with fire. The cleansing of earth and the heavens with fire is the "Fire" of His Wrath. God desires to purify them after the evil of Satan and men have had their time. The following scriptures will illustrate this.

Zeph. 1;18, and 3:8 18"Neither their silver nor their gold Shall be able to deliver them In the day of the LORD's wrath; But <u>the whole land shall be devoured By the fire of His jealousy</u>, For He will make speedy riddance Of all those who dwell in the land."   8 "'Therefore wait for Me," says the LORD, "Until the day I rise up for plunder; My determination *is* to gather the nations to My assembly of kingdoms, To pour on them My indignation, All My fierce anger; <u>All the earth shall be devoured With the fire of My jealousy</u>.'"

Nahum 1:2, 6 2 "God *is* jealous, and the LORD avenges; The LORD avenges and *is* furious. The LORD will take vengeance on His adversaries, And He <u>reserves *wrath* for His enemies</u>;" 6 "Who can stand before His indignation? And who can endure the fierceness of His anger? <u>His fury is poured out like fire</u>, And the rocks are thrown down by Him."

Other scriptures: Ps. 11:6, Ps. 97:3-5, Isa. 13:9. Further proof that God never intended for His Heavens and Earth to be totally annihilated lays in the next few verses:

Isa. 60:13,15. [14] "Also the sons of those who afflicted you Shall come bowing to you, And all those who despised you shall fall prostrate at the soles of your feet; And they shall call you The City of the LORD, Zion of the Holy One of Israel. [15] Whereas you have been forsaken and hated, So that no one went through *you*. I will make you an eternal excellence, A joy of many generations."

Jer. 33:19-21,25,26. [19] "And the word of the LORD came to Jeremiah, saying, [20] "Thus says the LORD: 'If you can break My covenant with the day and My covenant with the night, so that there will not be day and night in their season, [21] then My covenant may also be broken with David My servant, so that he shall not have a son to reign on his throne, and with the Levites, the priests, My ministers." [25] "Thus says the LORD: 'If My covenant *is* not with day and night, *and if* I have not appointed the ordinances of heaven and earth, [26] then I will cast away the descendants of Jacob and David My servant, *so* that I will not take *any* of his descendants *to be* rulers over the descendants of Abraham, Isaac, and Jacob. For I will cause their captives to return, and will have mercy on them."

[6] "For unto us a Child is born, Unto us a Son is given; And the government will be upon His shoulder. And His name will be called Wonderful, Counselor, Mighty God, Everlasting Father, Prince of Peace. [7] Of the increase of *His* government and peace *There will be* no end, Upon the throne of David and over His kingdom, To order it and establish it with judgment and justice From that time forward, even forever. The zeal of the Lord of hosts will perform this." Isa. 9:6,7

[15] "Then the seventh angel sounded: And there were loud voices in heaven, saying, "The kingdoms of this world have become *the kingdoms* of our Lord and of His Christ, and He shall reign forever and ever!'" Rev. 11:15

Note there are two cleansings of the earth and Heavens. The first time is a partial cleansing for the 1000 years, and then the second is the final grand renewal and replacing for eternity.

THE " BEMA" JUDGMENT SEAT

All of the Bride must appear before the Judgment Seat of Christ. They will receive judgment for the things done in the body whether good or bad. Rom. 14;10-12. Now there are to be three judgments by Jesus. The first will be the "Bema" Judgment Seat of Christ for His Bride, Church, or Body, this will be in Heaven. The second one will be Jesus' judgment of Israel, and then the Nations, and these will take place at the beginning of His 1000-year reign on earth. The third one will be the Great White Throne Judgment where all of the wicked dead will be raised to stand before Jesus at the end of the Millennium reign of Christ of earth. It is not clear just where this judgment will take place, most likely it will be in the heavens.

"Bema" comes from the name of the Greek Judge's Throne or Bench where they judged athletic contests and handed out laurel wreaths as rewards for the winners. Paul use this expression to reveal how all Christians will be judged and rewarded by Christ based on how well they served Him since they became believers. Now God has laid the foundation and if anyone builds on this foundation with gold, silver, precious stones, wood, hay, or straw each ones work will become manifest, for the Day will declare it, because it will be rewarded by fire, and fire will test each ones work, of what sort it is.

9 "For we are God's fellow workers; you are God's field, *you are* God's building. 10 According to the grace of God which was given to me, as a wise master builder I have laid the foundation, and another builds on it. But let each one take heed how he builds on it. 11 For no other foundation can anyone lay than that which is laid, which is Jesus Christ. 12 Now if anyone builds on this foundation *with* gold, silver, precious stones, wood, hay, straw, 13 each one's work will become clear; for the Day will declare it, because it will be revealed by fire; and the fire will test each one's work, of what sort it is. 14 If anyone's work which he has built on *it* endures, he will receive a reward. 15 If anyone's work is burned, he will suffer loss; but he himself will be saved, yet so as through fire." 1 Cor. 3: 9-15

Now the gold, silver, and precious stones will represent the valuable Spiritual work we allowed God to do through us. The wood, hay, and straw will show that work was done in our own strength, not Christ's. This judgment is not to punish but to reward faithful service. Some will receive crowns others will receive nothing because their works were "hay or stubble." All of these judgments are concerned with life's activities in light of eternity. The Bible gives no descriptions of the rewards Christ will give. Just know that we can be assured that what is received will be true and proper. What joy there will be as each is blessed one way or the other because we will know each has received his just dues.

Remember dear children the Lord has promised mansions, and crowns. We know there are at least five crowns, Crown of Life, Crown of Glory, Crown of rejoicing, a Crown Incorruptible or imperishable, and a Crown of Righteousness.

[24] "Do you not know that those who run in a race all run, but one receives the prize? Run in such a way that you may obtain *it*. [25] And everyone who competes *for the prize* is temperate in all things. Now they *do it* to obtain a perishable crown, but we *for* an imperishable *crown*. [26] Therefore I run thus: not with uncertainty. Thus I fight: not as *one who* beats the air. [27] But I discipline my body and bring *it* into subjection, lest, when I have preached to others, I myself should become disqualified." 1 Cor .9: 24-27

THE MARRIAGE SUPPER

Rev. 19:7-9, [7] "Let us be glad and rejoice and give Him glory, for <u>the marriage of the Lamb</u> has come, and <u>His wife has made herself ready</u>." [8] And to her it was granted to be arrayed in fine linen, clean and bright, for <u>the fine linen is the righteous acts</u> of the saints. [9] Then he said to me, 'Write: '<u>Blessed *are* those who are called to the marriage supper of the Lamb</u>!' And he said to me, These are the true sayings of God.'"

What can be said about Jesus' Marriage Supper, the scriptures say so little? Imagine Jesus' anticipation, how long it has been, and what Jesus has gone through for Him to come to this wonderful long planned ceremony. To sing and give praise for Jesus' works, that will go on eternally. To give Him credit for calling His Bride to Himself, that will continue throughout eternity. To know all of Jesus' love will take the Bride an eternity, and for this most exciting, blessed, loving occasion the Bride will be blessed eternally. This will most truly bless the heart of Jesus. Stop and think how much the Father has put into this marriage. It is a culmination of His desire in His Family planning. Jesus still has to bring Israel to judgment. There is much still ahead, but for now there is great joy in Heaven as Jesus finalizes this union. <u>The Heart of the Father must be blessed</u>!

<u>What is the Bride's heart like</u> in all of this? This is the great climax for the Bride; a celebration the likes of which Heaven and Earth has never seen! Can any child of God have any idea what will take place? Then consider this, assume The Father has given directions to His angels to set up the greatest Supper that Heaven have ever seen? Their work has been long in planning; a brand new building has already been completed. Yes a brand new special facility just for this Supper for thousands and thousands of Jesus' Bride and Marriage Supper guests, those who are called or invited. They will be souls of the tribulation martyrs and the Old Testament Saints. They are already in heaven because of the first rapture. This new facility will supply room for all the serving of food plus the space for all of the dancing and peripheral ceremonies and festivities. Just imagine the gold, the silver, the jewels and the fabulous furnishings, nothing similar has ever happened!

Father God is the Master of Ceremonies and He has withheld nothing from this joyous occasion, especially love. The outpouring of God's Love takes the breath away from even Jesus! Grace and Glory have freedom to flow throughout the entire area touching everyone over and over again! Heaven's Blessings and presents are distributed again and again. But what can the imaginations of man show about God's loving care?

THE SECOND COMING AND ARMAGEDDON

THE MESSIAH'S TRIUMPH AND KINGDOM

[1] "Why do the nations rage, And the people plot a vain thing? [2] <u>The kings of the earth set themselves, And the rulers take counsel together, Against the LORD and against His Anointed,</u> *saying,* [3] 'Let us break Their bonds in pieces And cast away Their cords from us.' [4] He who sits in the heavens shall laugh; The LORD shall hold them in derision. [5]   Then He shall speak to them in His wrath, And distress them in His deep displeasure." Psalm 2:1-5

The nations and Israel are the two occupants on earth after the Bride's disappearance, and there is also the adversary of them all Satan and his team. God has the stage set for man to openly seek his own demise. With the dedicated children of Jesus safely in Heaven God now allows the children of Israel and the nations their final time for choosing life or death. At the culmination of the Great Tribulation the stage is set for Jesus' return to earth. The seven Great Bowl Judgments are over and the nations have either joined the Kings of the East in their effort to throw off the rule of Antichrist or they will join the confederacy of the Antichrist.

[11] "Now I saw heaven opened, and behold, <u>a white horse. And He who sat on him *was* called Faithful and True, and in righteousness He judges and makes war.</u> [12] His eyes *were* like a flame of fire, and on His head *were* many crowns. He had a name written that no one knew except Himself. [13] He *was* clothed with a robe dipped in blood, and His name is called The Word of God. [14] <u>And the armies in heaven, clothed in fine linen, white and clean, followed Him on white horses.</u> [15] Now out of His mouth goes a sharp sword, that with it He should strike <u>the nations</u>. And He Himself will rule them with a rod of iron. He Himself treads the wine press of the fierceness and wrath of Almighty God. [16] And He has on *His* robe and on His thigh a name written." Rev. 19:11-16

Jesus comes out of Heaven with His Armies and His Bride, and He is ready to strike the nations who He will rule with a rod of iron. Notice He is to strike the nations not Israel and He rules them with a rod of iron not Israel. Also notice nothing is said about the emptying of Paradise* or the earth of the souls of the Old Testament Saints, or of all of the souls from Adam and Eve, or any of the men and women from those times who must follow the Bride, because they are coming down for the Judgment of Israel and the nations. Nothing is said about the Bride waging war or fighting because Jesus with the sword of His mouth and His Army's angels are capable of doing all that is needed.* With the exception of Matthew 24, this statement may be all that is needed to bring everyone to the judgment.

29 "Immediately after the tribulation of those days the sun will be darkened, and the moon will not give its light, the stars will fall from heaven, and the powers of the heavens will be shaken. "then the sign of the Son of Man will appear in heaven, and then all the tribes of the earth will mourn, and they will see the Son of Man coming on the clouds of heaven with power and great glory. And He will send His angels with a great sound of a trumpet, and they will gather together His elect from the four winds, from one end of heaven to the other." Matt. 24:29-31

14 "For they are spirits of demons, performing signs, *which* go out to the kings of the earth and of the whole world, to gather them to the battle of that great day of God Almighty. 'Behold I am coming as a thief. Blessed is he who watches, and keeps his garments, lest he walk naked and they see his shame.' 16 And they gathered them together to the place called in Hebrew, Armageddon. 17 Then the seventh angel poured out his bowl into the air, and a loud voice came out of the temple of heaven, from the throne, saying, '**It is done**!' 18 And there were noises and thundering and lightning; and there was a great earthquake, such a mighty and great earthquake as had not occurred since men were on the earth. 19 Now the great city was divided into three parts, and the cities of the nations fell. And great Babylon was remembered before God, to give her the cup of the wine of the fierceness of His wrath. 20 Then every island fled away, and the mountains were not found. 21 And great hail from heaven fell

upon men, *each hailstone* about the weight of a talent. Men blasphemed God because of the plague of the hail, since that plague was exceedingly great." Rev. 16:14-21

17 "Then I saw an angel standing in the sun; and he cried with a loud voice, saying to all the birds that fly in the midst of heaven, 'Come and gather together for the supper of the great God, 18 that you may eat the flesh of kings, the flesh of captains, the flesh of mighty men, the flesh of horses and of those who sit on them, and the flesh of all *people,* free and slave, both small and great.' 19 And I saw the beast, the kings of the earth, and their armies, gathered together to make war against Him who sat on the horse and against His army. 20 Then the beast was captured, and with him the false prophet who worked signs in his presence, by which he deceived those who received the mark of the beast and those who worshiped his image. These two were cast alive into the lake of fire burning with brimstone. 21 And the rest were killed with the sword proceeded from the mouth of Him who sat on the horse. And all the birds were filled with their flesh." Rev. 19:17-21

This will be the greatest mobilization of the armies of all the nations that the world would ever see. The armies of the East soon meet with Antichrist and his hordes, together they turn to fight Jesus and His Armies of heaven. The battle is soon over and all the earth is stilled and ready for the end of the cleansing work of God Himself for the King has arrived.

THE SECOND MAN RISING
IS JESUS

Jesus' work starts at His birth but there is a new beginning after his resurrection as men become born again, and when the first men receive the Holy Spirit and have adequate teaching in the work of the Spirit allowing Jesus to come into and abide with men. This "Jesus Rising" in men starts the first time in the disciples, before His ascension, [John 20:22] and then it will overflow throughout the time of the Gentiles until all men who are saved are filled with Jesus. The Second Man Rising then is a continuous ongoing move of Jesus in all men who will receive the born again experience. This will occur at anytime from the time of the Gentile's beginning until the final reception of God Himself at the end of the Millennium. Jesus abiding in man is first written of in John 6:56 and then there are others that also says man has Jesus abiding in him.

Other scriptures that speak of that same subject are:

10 ". . .that in the dispensation of the fullness of the times He might gather together <u>in one all things in Christ</u>, both which are in heaven and which are on earth in Him." Eph. 1:10

17 ". . .that <u>Christ may dwell in your hearts through faith</u>; that you, being rooted and grounded in love, 18 may be able to comprehend with all the saints what *is* the width and length and depth and height— 19 to know the love of Christ which passes knowledge; that <u>you may be filled with all the fullness of God</u>." Eph. 3:17—19

10 "He who descended is also the One who ascended far above all the heavens, that <u>He might fill all things</u>." Eph. 4:10

19 "For it pleased *the Father that* <u>in Him all the fullness should dwell</u>, 20 and by Him to reconcile all things to Himself, by Him, whether things on earth or things in heaven, having made peace through the blood of His cross." Col. 1:19,20

9 "For in Him dwells <u>all the fullness of the Godhead</u> bodily; 10 and <u>you are complete in Him</u>, who is the head of all principality and power." Col. 2:9,10

10 ". . .and have put on the new *man* who is renewed in knowledge according to the image of Him who created him, 11 where there is neither Greek nor Jew, circumcised nor uncircumcised, barbarian, Scythian, slave *nor* free, but <u>Christ *is* all and in all</u>." Col. 3:10,11

This then is the work of Jesus, to gather all men together in Him in preparation for the completion of His work in the earth, that will come at the final time of the earth training of men.

PAUSE AND REFLECT

The first 2000 years of Jesus has been devoted to bringing Jesus' Bride into being. The whole struggle of the church to survive has brought forth just the children of God that will have hearts prepared and open to the Holy Spirit, and hearts that will prove true to God's Plan for these times. The Bride will have made the transition into the Spirit Realm for which Jesus has worked. Now the Bride has the task of walking in the reality of the Spirit world on earth for a thousand years learning how to grow closer to Jesus and the Father's ways. The church will be walking on the replenished earth and living as a Spirit-filled Being following God's Heavenly Ways!

CHAPTER FIVE

JUDGMENT TO JUDGMENT
JUDGMENT IN PROPHESY

God does nothing pertaining to His children that He hasn't described for them in His Bible. In regards to <u>His time of judging</u> all of His children, He has set these scriptures before us that we should have understanding of His actions and know the why of them, that <u>men's hearts are either for God or for Self.</u> There are three major times of Judgment on the children of the earth. <u>FIRST JUDGMENT</u>, He will bring His first Wife "<u>Israel</u>" before His chosen Judge, His Son. <u>SECOND JUDGMENT</u>, He will bring the children of "<u>The Nations of the World</u>" before Christ's judgment. <u>THIRD JUDGMENT</u>, The last one, will be for "<u>All Men</u>" <u>who have thoroughly unrepentant hearts.</u> The Son of God completes His final and most hurtful Task "The Great White Throne Judgment" with the final condemnation of all the lost children who refused to accept Him as their Savior and God.

THE TIME OF THE JUDGMENTS

With the gathering of His Elect, Jesus is bringing all of Israel before Him to be judged. The Angels will gather all Israel from their graves, from

Abraham's Bosom, and all those who lived through and survived the Tribulation.

11 "And from the time *that* the daily *sacrifice* is taken away, and the abomination of desolation is set up, *there shall be* one thousand two hundred and ninety days. 12 Blessed *is* he who waits, and comes to the one thousand three hundred and thirty-five days." Daniel 12:11,12.

This is the source of the 45-day judgment period, Daniel 12. Daniel gives 1290 days after the abomination [that is the mid-tribulation or 3 1\2 years until the end of the tribulation]. Then it is said that blessed are those who come to the 1335 days. This indicates a 45-day time span that something good is going to happen. One of the blessing is Israel will be saved in one day. If Israel is judged in one day then there are 44 days left with no explanation. Assumption is made that this is the time all other people are judged, the people from the time of Adam to Noah, the ones from Noah to Abraham, and all those on through the tribulation. The exceptions are the Bride of Christ and all the lost and wicked who is reserved for the Great White Throne Judgment.

JUDGMENT OF ISRAEL

Most assuredly, I say to you, the hour is coming. and now is, when the dead will hear the voice of the Son of God; and those who hear will live. For as the Father has life in Himself, so He has granted the Son to have life in Himself, and has given Him authority to execute judgment also, because He is the Son of Man. Do not marvel at this; for the hour is coming in which all who are in the graves will hear His voice and come forth—those who have done good, to the resurrection of life, and those who have done evil, to the resurrection of condemnation. John 5: 25-29

Father God has given His Son authority* to execute Judgment, and Jesus, the Son of God will be the Judge of Israel, and of all the children of the earth that have ever lived in separate times. Israel is the first nation to be judged after Jesus' return. After Armageddon Jesus sets His Throne in Jerusalem and from there He will judge first the Tribes of Israel. *John 5:22

Immediately after the tribulation of those days the sun will be darkened, and the moon will not give it's light; the stars will fall from heaven, and the powers of the heaven will be shaken. Then the sign of the Son of Man will appear in heaven, and then <u>all the *tribes of the earth</u> will mourn, and they will see the Son of Man coming on the clouds of heaven with power and great glory. And He will send His angels with a great sound of a trumpet, and they will <u>gather together His *Elect</u> from the four winds, from one end of heaven to the other. Matt.24: 29-31 *Israel. For an explanation of Elect see Rom. 11:5-7.

With the gathering of His Elect Jesus is bringing <u>all of Israel</u> before Him to be judged. The Angels will gather <u>all Israel</u> from their graves, from Abraham's Bosom, and all those who lived through and survived the Tribulation. Ezekiel prophesied the ultimate restoration and the bringing of the ten tribes of Israel and the two tribes of Judah together during the time of their captivity in Babylon. There will be no longer be ten "Lost Tribes."

11 "Then He said to me, "Son of man, these bones are <u>the whole house of Israel</u>. They indeed say, 'Our bones are dry, our hope is lost, and we ourselves are cut off!' 12 Therefore prophesy and say to them, 'Thus says the Lord GOD: "Behold, O My people, I will open your graves and cause you to come up from your graves, and <u>bring you into the land of Israel</u>. 13 Then you shall know that I *am* the LORD, when I have opened your graves, O My people, and brought you up from your graves. <u>14 I will put My Spirit in you, and you shall live, and I will place you in your own land.</u> Then you shall know that I, the LORD, have spoken *it* and performed *it*', says the LORD." Ezekiel 37:11-14. Note this is only Israel coming out of the graves.

20 "In those days and in that time, says the LORD, <u>'The iniquity of Israel shall be sought, but *there shall be* none</u>; And <u>the sins of Judah, but they shall not be found</u>; For I will pardon those whom I preserve.'" Jeremiah 50:20.

9 "'For behold, the stone That I have laid before Joshua: Upon the stone *are* seven eyes. Behold, I will engrave its inscription,' Says the LORD of hosts, 'And <u>I will remove the iniquity of that land in one day</u>. 10In that

day,' says the LORD of hosts, 'Everyone will invite his neighbor Under his vine and under his fig tree.'" Zech. 3:9,10. * Eyes of the Lord. Zech. 4:10.

The Father's love for Israel is so profound that He desired to spare them from the tensions of a long trial period; He gave them who had done well a new heart in one day! In the following scriptures there are several remarkable statements made. The resurrected David will be their King, The Messiah Jesus will be their shepherd, and all Israel will be obedient, an everlasting [New] covenant is made with Israel, God's sanctuary will be in their midst forevermore, they shall dwell there, they, their children, and their children's children, forever! This means that the people of Israel will be having children forever! [They are not in Heaven living like the angels].

This means that Israel will not only be living through the Millennium, but also they will enter the promised NEW EARTH FOREVER in all of it's wonderful Remade, Rebuilt, Regenerated, GOD CREATED ETERNAL BLESSINGS. This is not the end of the wonders in this scripture, it clearly says that the Nations will know because they will also be there in their midst forever! In Geneses 15:5 God said to Abram "Look now toward the heaven, and count the stars if you are able to number them." And then He said, "So shall your descendants be." In the heavens that man now knows about, this number is not even imagined to be countable! It is obvious that God was not talking about Israel filling the earth with this family because the earth could not hold them [remember once born in the Kingdom of God the children will never die] Now let's think of the implications here mentioned! [This will be addressed in the last chapter]

24 "David My servant *shall be* king over them, and they shall all have one shepherd; they shall also walk in My judgments and observe My statutes, and do them. 25 Then they shall dwell in the land that I have given to Jacob My servant, where your fathers dwelt; and they shall dwell there, they, their children, and their children's children, forever; and My servant David *shall be* their prince forever. 26 Moreover I will make a covenant of peace with them, and it shall be an everlasting covenant with them; I will establish them and multiply them, and I will set My sanctuary in their midst forevermore. 27 My tabernacle also shall be with them;

indeed I will be their God, and they shall be My people. [28] The nations also will know that I, the LORD, sanctify Israel, when My sanctuary is in their midst forevermore." Ezekiel 37:24-28

The Messiah Jesus will be their shepherd, and all Israel will be obedient, the Lord's sanctuary will be in their midst, and the nations will know. What a blessing the Lord's rewards are, and what a reward has God's Judgment turned out to be! Note: Isa. 11:11,12; Jere. 23:3,4,6. Zech. 8:11,12. From all of these scriptures the true meaning of who "The Remnant," that is saved and brought into the millennium, will be made quite clear. Not all of Israel is "saved," only the remnant who's Hearts are found to be true lovers of God and their Messiah, the rest of Israel's hearts were hardened. Rom. 11: 1-8

RESTORATION OF THE EARTH AND ISRAEL

And that He may send Jesus Christ, who was preached to you before, [21] "Whom heaven must receive until the times of restoration of all things, which God has spoken by the mouth of all His holy prophets since the world began." Acts 3:20,21

Man's occupation of earth since the flood has done nothing to preserve or restore the earth. Man's occupation has only contributed to the destructive pollution of the earth's eco system. Man has failed totally as the steward of the planet. The final blow to this destruction will come from the ravages of Satan's seven years, further devastating the earth's fragile ecological systems.

[18] "The nations were angry, and Your wrath has come, And the time of the dead, that they should be judged, And that You should reward Your servants the prophets and the saints, And those who fear Your name, small and great, And should destroy those who destroy the earth." Rev. 11:18.

For God's children to return and live again as they should required the Father to renew the earth, Christ will bring a healing cleansing to all the wounds of this worlds past mistreatment.

Then he brought me back to the door of the temple; and there was water, flowing from under the threshold of the temple toward the east, for the front of the temple faced east; the water was flowing from under the right side of the temple, south of the altar. ^{9} "And it shall be _that every living thing that moves, wherever the rivers go, will live._ There will be a very great multitude of fish, because these waters go there; <u>for they will be healed</u>, and everything will live wherever the river goes. ^{10} It shall be _that_ fishermen will stand by it from En Gedi to En Eglaim; they will be _places_ for spreading their nets. Their fish will be of the same kinds as the fish of the Great Sea, exceedingly many. ^{11} But its swamps and marshes will not be healed; they will be given over to salt. ^{12} Along the bank of the river, on this side and that, will grow <u>all _kinds of_ trees used for food;</u> their leaves will not wither, and their fruit will not fail. They will bear fruit every month, because their water flows from the sanctuary. Their fruit will be for food, and their leaves for medicine." Ezekiel 47:1, 8-12.

^{2} "The Spirit of the LORD shall rest upon Him, The <u>Spirit of wisdom and understanding, The Spirit of counsel and might</u>, The Spirit of knowledge and of the fear of the LORD. ^{3} His delight _is_ in the fear of the LORD, And He shall not judge by the sight of His eyes, Nor decide by the hearing of His ears; ^{4} But with <u>righteousness He shall judge the poor</u>, And decide with equity for the meek of the earth; <u>He shall strike the earth with the rod of His mouth</u>, And with the breath of His lips <u>He shall slay the wicked</u>. ^{5} Righteousness shall be the belt of His loins, And faithfulness the belt of His waist." Isaiah 11:2-4, 11-16

During the thousand years limited sin will be shown through man, but evil expressed will be dealt with immediately by Christ's ruling with "a rod of iron" for He shall slay the wicked ones. Once Satan is cast into the fiery lake at the end of the millennium Sin will never exist again. God's transforming of Men and Women's hearts will be the final cleansing of sin from the Universe. Israel will finally become a light to the Nations, the Gentiles. Isa. 42:6. Israel will enter into all the blessings of the Promised Land, and they will live in the peace that escaped them so many times in their turbulent past.

God's past covenant blessings with Israel will finally be given their true expression.

2 "<u>I will make you a great nation</u>; I will bless you And <u>make your name great</u>; And you shall be a blessing. 3 I will bless those who bless you, And I will curse him who curses you; <u>And in you all the families of the earth shall be blessed.</u>" Gen. 12:2,3.

10 "Yet <u>the number of the children of Israel Shall be as the sand of the sea</u>, Which cannot be measured or numbered. And it shall come to pass In the place where it was said to them, 'You *are* not My people,' *There* it shall be said to them, '<u>*You are* sons of the living God</u>. Come, and let us return to the LORD; For He has torn, but He will heal us; He has stricken, but He will bind us up.'" 2 "After two days He will revive us; On the third day He will raise us up, that we may live in His sight. 3 Let us know, Let us pursue the knowledge of the LORD. His going forth is established as the morning; He will come to us like the rain, Like the latter *and* former rain to the earth." Hosea 1:10, 6:1-3.

JUDGMENT OF THE NATIONS

There are questions about who are to be judged during the 44 days left in Zechariah's prophecy. Assumption is made that all men from Adam's time until the end of the tribulation must be considered because no other Judgments seem to be given than the ones for this time. Therefore the groups of men from Adam to Noah, Noah to Abraham and Abraham to Moses will be the subjects of this inquiry. The Adam to Noah group came into disfavor with God and all were put into prison. This prison was in the earth [the reason for this place of confinement is Satan owed the earth and it was not legal for God to remove from earth what didn't belong to Him. Adam had given the earth over to Satan by his disobedience to God]. There aren't any scriptures showing the removal of these people.

1 Peter 3:18-20

18 "For Christ also suffered once for sins, the just for the unjust, that He might bring us to God, being put to death in the flesh but made alive by

the Spirit, [19] by whom also He went and preached to the spirits in prison, [20] who formerly were disobedient, when once the Divine longsuffering waited in the days of Noah, while *the* ark was being prepared, in which a few, that is, eight souls, were saved through water."

No scripture indicates that they were removed from earth or what Jesus said to them. The fact that many people of that time were greatly loved by God requires an answer to what will God do with them?

Jude 10-15

[10] "But these speak evil of whatever they do not know; and whatever they know naturally, like brute beasts, in these things they corrupt themselves. [11] Woe to them! For they have gone in the way of Cain, have run greedily in the error of Balaam for profit, and perished in the rebellion of Kora [12] These are spots in your love feasts, while they feast with you without fear, serving *only* themselves. *They are* clouds without water, carried about by the winds; late autumn trees without fruit, twice dead, pulled up by the roots; [13] raging waves of the sea, foaming up their own shame; wandering stars for whom is reserved the blackness of darkness forever. [14] Now Enoch, the seventh from Adam, prophesied about these men also, saying, "Behold, the Lord comes with ten thousands of His saints, [15] to execute judgment on all, to convict all who are ungodly among them of all their ungodly deeds which they have committed in an ungodly way, and of all the harsh things which ungodly sinners have spoken against Him.""

Jude is referring to the souls in the time of Adam to Noah. "The Lord comes with His Saints" indicates the time of His second coming or the Judgment time after His coming and it is clearly shown what happens to the ungodly men of that time. The following verses show what happens to all the rest of the good men.

Matthew 12:33-37

Either make the tree good and its fruit good, or else make the tree bad and its fruit bad; for a tree is known by its fruit. Brood of vipers! How can you, being evil, speak good things? For out of the abundance of the heart the mouth speaks. A good man out of the good treasure of his heart brings forth good things, and an evil man out of the evil treasure brings forth evil things. But I say to you that for every idle word men speak, <u>they will give account of it in the day of judgment.</u> For by your words you will <u>be justified</u>, and by your words you will be condemned."

This scripture addresses a day of judgment and "the good man and the evil man" as the ones to be judged. This doesn't refer to Israel only. The only two times judgment is called for is during the 45 days after the tribulation and after Christ's 1000-year reign on earth when the Great White Throne Judgment is convened. [Omitting of course the judgment of Christ's Bride] With that under consideration, the assumption is made all of the "to be judged of the world" will have to be brought up at this time. There is the question of the Gentiles that survived the tribulation and of the Gentiles that have died in all of the past ages. When will they be raised up? Perhaps this is the scripture and this is the time for all these Gentiles.

Note, all those that come before the Great White Throne will have already been self-judged to eternal damnation and these scriptures cover basically the time and rules of God's judgment for all other groups of the Bible that has been mentioned.

John 3:18-21

<u>He who believes in Him is not condemned</u>; but he who does not believe is condemned already, because he has not believed in the name of the only begotten Son of God. And this is the condemnation, that the light has come into the world, and men loved darkness rather than light, because their deeds were evil. For everyone practicing evil hates the light and does not come to the light, lest his deeds may be clearly seen, that they have been done in God.

This statement implies all Christians [they believe in the light] will not be judged and all others will be condemned. John 5:24 makes it clear that there is no condemning judgment, there is no death, and there is eternal life for all who are born-again. It is understood from this scripture if someone hears about Jesus and ignores it, that they have condemned themselves to everlasting damnation and therefore set themselves up before the Great White Throne for Jesus to complete their eternal condemnation. Here are scriptures that give God leeway in judging whomsoever He wills because of Jesus' shed blood.

Romans 2:6,7; 10-16

6 ". . .who *"will render to each one according to his deeds"*: 7 eternal life to those who by patient continuance in doing good seek for glory, honor, and immortality. . ." 10 ". . .but glory, honor, and peace to everyone who works what is good, to the Jew first and also to the Greek. 11 For there is no partiality with God. 12 For as many as have sinned without law will also perish without law, and as many as have sinned in the law will be judged by the law 13 (for not the hearers of the law *are* just in the sight of God, but the doers of the law will be justified; 14 for when Gentiles, who do not have the law, by nature do the things in the law, these, although not having the law, are a law to themselves, 15 who show the work of the law written in their hearts, their conscience also bearing witness, and between themselves *their* thoughts accusing or else excusing *them*) 16 in the day when God will judge the secrets of men by Jesus Christ, according to my gospel."

THE BRIDE'S WORK

The destiny of the Church is to rule with Christ forever.

11 "This is a faithful saying: For if we died with *Him*, We shall also live with *Him*. 12 If we endure, We shall also reign with *Him*. If we deny *Him*, He also will deny us." 11 Timothy 2:11,12

This time of 1000 years just ahead of us has very special assignments to be given to God's People. Israel will be in new bodies with new hearts and their task is to learn how to live in the environment of Israel's King on Earth. Just so the Bride of Christ has learning and growing period. They will be on earth living in a fortress camp outside of Jerusalem [Rev.

20:9] Their assignments will come from Jesus the Reigning King, and will be to assist Him in controlling the Nations of the Earth with an iron scepter [rod] of iron.

"And he who overcomes, and keeps My works until the end, to him I will give power over the nations—<u>He shall rule them with a rod of iron</u>: As the potter's vessels shall be broken to pieces—as I also have received from My Father." Revelation 2:26,27.

The Bride will be given tasks of control and governing, so as to develop and grow in the ways of the Spirit, learning by doing all that Christ the King desires. The fact that the Bride will be given a new body and a new life like Jesus doesn't mean all are able to live and do everything perfectly without learning how to be able to use their new Spiritual body. Having the mind and body of Christ does not imply all the abilities to use them and be like Him are instantly present. God has set this interim time of 1000 years for several purposes. To teach and train Israel in the ways of their fathers, to give development and growth time for Jesus' new Bride, and to bring forth out of the Nations children of worth for the New Earth and the New Heavens. This combined schooling for Israel and the Bride will also bring to the Father the last acceptable family of children for His Eternal Family. This then is the reason and work required, train Israel in their new position as ruling Nation over all the Nations of the Earth, train the Bride of Christ to be more like Him, and bring forth from Israel and the Nations the final gathering of God's Eternal Family.

This is a time for all of God's children to draw closer to each other, a time of rest and peace, a time for growing in love for one another, a time for every child of God to appreciate a loving Father showing His love in many new ways to His children. The scriptures teach the destiny of the Church is to rule with Christ for the Millennium, and forever in the coming New Earth! The vision given John when he was lifted up to heaven was of 24 thrones, with 24 Elders sitting, clothed in white robes, with Crowns of Gold on their heads. Rev. 4:4 These Elders are the crowned representatives of the Church and Israel sitting on thrones as rulers under Jesus—Messiah—King.

"His Lord said to him, 'Well done, good and faithful servant; you have been faithful over a few things, <u>I will make you ruler over many things</u>.' Enter into the joy of the Lord." Matthew 25:23

"And he said to him, 'Well done, good servant; because you were faithful in a very little, <u>have authority over ten cities</u>.'" Luke 19:17

"If we endure, <u>we shall also reign with *Him*</u>. If we deny *Him*, He also will deny us." 2 Timothy 2:12

4 "And I saw thrones, and they sat on them, and judgment was committed to them. Then *I saw* the souls of those who had been beheaded for their witness to Jesus and for the word of God, who had not worshiped the beast or his image, and had not received *his* mark on their foreheads or on their hands. <u>And they lived and reigned with Christ for a thousand years.</u>" Revelation 20:4

Note: Revelation 20 is also saying not only The Bride of Christ will reign during this time but the tribulation saints will also participate in reigning over the Nations.

SATAN, THE OLD SERPENT

The Battle of Armageddon ends Satan's reign, and then his sin is lifted out of the earth when he is defeated and finally bound for a thousand years. Ezekiel's vision of the millennium shows restoration of the planet taking place; there is a blessing with Satan's departure.

It was an angel descending from heaven with the key of the Abyss [The bottomless pit, the center of the Earth; bottomless implies the only way out was up] This angel had a great chain in his hand and then he gripped and overpowered the old serpent, the devil and Satan, and bound him for a thousand years, then hurled him into the Abyss and closed and sealed it stopping Satan's evil works until the thousand years are up.

Satan is used one last time to help complete the sifting of men to find the ones <u>who's hearts are not right with God</u>. He will be used to deceive, seduce, and lead astray all men in the Nations who will follow Him. They will be like the sands of the sea and they go to war against God's people the saints who are camped outside the beloved city, however fire will descend from heaven and consume them. When Satan has completed this one last task he is finally hurled into the fiery lake of burning brimstone where he will be tormented day and night [all of the time] forever and ever through all ages without end.

GREAT WHITE THRONE JUDGMENT

JUDGING THE SOULS OF UNREPEN-TANT SINNERS

11 "Then I saw a <u>great white throne</u> and Him who sat on it, from whose face the earth and the heaven fled away. And there was found no place for them. 12 And I saw the dead, small and great, standing before God, and books were opened. And another book was opened, which is *The Book of Life*. And <u>the dead were judged</u> <u>according to their works</u>, by the things which were written in the books." Revelation 20:11-12

There is for every lost soul a final time to come before their Savior and Creator. All truth will display its self to those who are given bodies to stand before Jesus Christ. No other people will stand before Him except unrepentant sinners. They will be standing at their judgment in their newly resurrected bodies that cannot die, and at their trial the books will be opened about their deeds done in the flesh, and another book, *The Book of Life*, will be checked so no error will be committed. Considering the final enormity of this trials conclusion, God especially does not want to see anyone misjudged!

13 "The <u>sea gave up the dead</u> who were in it, and <u>Death and Hades deliv-ered up the dead</u> who were in them. And they were judged, <u>each one according to his works</u>. 14 Then Death and Hades were cast into the lake of fire. This is the second death. 15 <u>And anyone not found written in *The Book of Life* was cast into the lake of fire.</u>" Revelation 20:13-15

The sea referred to here means <u>the sea of all humanity</u> who are unrepen-tant sinners left still alive on earth along with all those in Death and Hades, everyone will be given eternal bodies to stand before their Judge. Then everyone will be cast into the lake of fire. This judgment is only <u>the final display of what was done in their flesh</u> that was to their great loss. All who are called there have already been judged before they appeared in this court!

THIRD MAN RISING

THIRD MAN RISING IS GOD

ENTERING ALL MEN

[20] "But now Christ is risen from the dead, *and* has become the first fruits of those who have fallen asleep. [21] For since by man *came* death, by Man also *came* the resurrection of the dead. [22] For as in Adam all die, even so <u>in Christ all shall be made alive.</u> [23] But each one in his own order: Christ the first fruits, afterward those *who are* Christ's at His coming. [24] <u>Then *comes* the end, when He delivers the kingdom to God the Father,</u> when He puts an end to all rule and all authority and power. [25] For He must reign till He has put all enemies under His feet. [26] The last enemy *that* will be destroyed *is* death. [27] For '*He has put all things under His feet."* But when He says "all things are put under *Him,'* it is evident that He who put all things under Him is excepted. [28] Now when all things are made subject to Him, then the Son Himself will also be subject to Him who put all things under Him, <u>that God may be all in all</u>." 1 Cor.15:20-28

Nothing could sum up this marvelous work of Jesus and the Father any better than this scripture above. What a perfect way to enter ETERNITY with Our Heavenly Father permanently indwelling every child of His. What an unbelievable union making our position a place of forever with Him right inside of us!

ETERNITY BEGINS

God doesn't teach that the old heavens and earth will be annihilated or destroyed by fire, only that the fire of His wrath will cover and clear out evil and the unwanted of the earth and the lower heaven of Satan's realm. Jerusalem will always be just where it has always been. However there will be a renewing and massive changes taking place when God restores and makes like new the heaven and the earth. How could this great change take place? Only God knows He has never shown the how to His people. You should be assured that all that God will do when that time comes will be done so well that He makes it <u>His home with His children</u>.

Now I saw a <u>new heaven and a new earth</u>, for the first heaven and the first earth had passed away. Also there was no more <u>sea.</u>* 2 "Then I, John, saw <u>the holy city, New Jerusalem, coming down out of heaven from God</u>, prepared as a bride adorned for her husband. 3 And I heard a loud voice from heaven saying, "Behold, <u>the tabernacle of God *is* with men, and He will dwell with them</u>, and they shall be His people. <u>God Himself will be with them *and be* their God</u>. 4 And God will wipe away every tear from their eyes; there shall be no more death, nor sorrow, nor crying. There shall be no more pain, for the former things have passed away." 5 Then He who sat on the throne said, "Behold, I make <u>all things</u> new." And He said to me, "Write, for these words are true and faithful." 6 And He said to me, "It is done! I am the Alpha and the Omega, the Beginning and the End. I will give of the fountain of the water of life freely to him who thirsts. 7 He who overcomes <u>shall inherit all things</u>, and I will be his God and he shall be My son. 8 But the cowardly, unbelieving, abominable, murderers, sexually immoral, sorcerers, idolaters, and all liars shall have their part in the lake which burns with fire and brimstone, which is the second death." Rev.21:1-8 * The "no more sea" means no more sea of humanity, verse 8 describes the sea of humanity.

These scriptures tell his children that there will be a new heaven and a new earth. It also shows that only the lower heaven that Satan and his principalities and powers dwelt in are to be restored. He further tells of His gift of a New Jerusalem being sent down for His children. It is to hover the earth and be the permanent dwelling place of the Bride of Christ. This word also tells that God will dwell with them, indicating the changes that will be made are of an extraordinarily wonderful kind. God doesn't teach that the old heavens and earth will be annihilated only that they will be made like new.

In the opening of eternity, My hand will be shown to My love ones as never before. As I change, alter, and renew My heaven and earth I will be recreating an environment like none other. This is a very meaningful time and occasion to Me because Our relationship by then will have finally culminated into the opening stages of Our Family Time of Forever. My heart will be blessed as never before, and it is Our desire to bless Our completed Family by such works of wonder that they will become the beginning of your never ending blessings of life forever with Us.

Yes, the new earth will be so enhanced and lovely, not just like Eden of the Starting, but so much greater and more wonderful in every respect. The earth's entire environment will sustain complete renewing and cleansing. The air, water, and earth will never again be diminishing for the laws of thermodynamics will not be obedient to the ways of the past. [He showed a small bit of this during Moses' 40 years in the wilderness, the children's shoes, clothes, etc. didn't wear out] All of the basic science that man has become familiar with is part of My complete reworking and restoring. I will prepare all new laws of creation to be more conducive and agreeable to the plans for My future with My Family in My Universe.

 Oh My dear ones, I cannot reveal all because what I keep back from you now will become so much greater than the simple description I could pass on to you in words of your understanding. Just know that the little here revealed is My release of things contained, just to bless you with a picture of wonders everlasting. Come and be My ones of understanding, accepting the thoughts here exposed as just a peek of your heaven with Me.

Yes, you will have much more than the finest of your present imaginations ability to visualize a new creation of your earth, making everything that is presently in it so much more enhanced as to take your breath away with it's untellable beauty. Places with streets of gold, but many more expressions of wealth as to "boggle your mind." The peace, beauty and wonders of the earth's new mountains, hills, valleys, and seas of water, large and small, and of spots of wonders not yet imagined. Come now dear ones and use this little that is here given as incentive enough to have you become My source of truth to all My lost children that are around you now. These books are only to help you become the best salesmen and women of Our coming wonders. Will you submit to all I've called for you to do, and become the most blessed children of Mine?

REMEMBER GOD IN YOU THE HOPE OF GLORY

WILL YOU BE THE SALT OF THE EARTH

UNTIL ALL THIS COMES ABOUT?

The Glories Series
and
Other Books
by
Scott E. Beemer

Studies for Mature Christian Living
BOOK ONE—**SONRISE GLORIES**
Jesus in You
BOOK TWO—**MORNING GLORIES**
Holy Spirit's Morning Journal
BOOK THREE—**ETERNAL GLORIES**
Holy Spirit's Morning Journal
BOOK FOUR—**BELOVED GLORIES**
Holy Spirit's Poems and Proverbs
BOOK FIVE—**LOVABLE GLORIES**
Holy Spirit's Love Notes
BOOK SIX—**GLOWING GLORIES**
Holy Spirit's Journal Notes
BOOK SEVEN—**END TIME GLORIES**
Covenants to Eternity
BOOK EIGHT—**SEEKER'S GLORIES**
Holy Spirit's Seeker's Guide
BOOK NINE—**DYNAMIC GLORIES**
Holy Spirit's Teaching Manual #1
BOOK TEN—**ENDLESS GLORIES**
Holy Spirit's Teaching Manual #2
BOOK ELEVEN—**TRINITY GLORIES**
Holy Spirit's Teaching Manual #3
BOOK TWELVE—**HEAVEN'S GLORIES**
Holy Spirit's Teaching Manual #4
(Last in the Series)

GOD TALK
Beyond Believing, Just Knowing
LOVE TALK
Volume 1 and 2

You can order these through your favorite bookstore,
or to order direct, contact,

BLACK FOREST PRESS
488 Mountain View Drive
Mosheim, TN 37818
1423-422-4711
You may also order from the shopping cart on Web site
www.mindtreebooks.com

To contact Scott Beemer write to:
GOD'S OPEN FORUM
P.O. Box 80786
San Diego, CA 92138-0786
You may order Scott's Books at this Web site.
www.itsbeensold.com and
www.scottebeemer.com

Printed in the United States
58631LVS00003B/175-222